Peter Kinderman is Professor of Clinical Psychology at the
University of Liverpool. He studied Natural Sciences at King's
College, Cambridge before qualifying as a clinical psychologist
from Leeds University. After working in the NHS as a clinical
psychologist, Peter obtained a PhD from the University of
Liverpool, where he studied how people's paranoid delusional
beliefs were associated with their self-esteem and how they
explained events in their lives. Peter's research activity and
clinical work concentrate on understanding and helping people
with serious and enduring mental health problems, and on how
psychological science can assist public policy in health and
social care.

Peter has served twice as Chair of the British Psychological
Society's Division of Clinical Psychology and has been
involved in a wide range of discussions of mental health issues
with policy-makers and in the media.

THE NEW LAWS OF PSYCHOLOGY

Peter Kinderman

Professor of Clinical Psychology,
University of Liverpool

Constable & Robinson Ltd
55–56 Russell Square
London WC1B 4HP
www.constablerobinson.com

First published in the UK by Robinson,
an imprint of Constable & Robinson Ltd, 2014

A copy of the British Library Cataloguing in
Publication data is available from the British Library

This book is not intended as a substitute for medical advice or
treatment. Any person with a condition requiring medical attention
should consult a qualified medical practitioner or suitable therapist.

ISBN 978-1-78033-600-8 (trade paperback)
ISBN 978-1-78033-601-5 (ebook)

Printed and bound by CPI Group (UK) Ltd, Croydon, CR0 4YY

1 3 5 7 9 10 8 6 4 2

CONTENTS

Acknowledgements   vii
Introduction   ix

1   Are we controlled by our brains?   1
2   The old laws of psychology   30
3   The new laws of psychology: psychology at the
     heart of everything   66
4   Thinking differently: diagnosis   93
5   Thinking differently: well-being   141
6   Thinking differently: therapy   170
7   Master of your fate, captain of your soul   208

     Notes   219
     Index   231

ACKNOWLEDGEMENTS

I would like to thank everybody with whom I have shared ideas about this book, and who has helped me by reading and commenting upon earlier drafts. In particular, I would like to thank members of my family, who have been both insightful and patient, and who have helped me enormously in expressing my ideas appropriately. I would particularly like to thank Jen Tomkins and Anne Cooke, whose comments have been very influential in shaping the book, although I'm aware that I have discussed these ideas with very many more people – unfortunately too many to name individually. I am, of course, enormously grateful to Fritha Saunders, Jamie Joseph, Charlotte Macdonald and all at Constable & Robinson who have helped make this book possible.

INTRODUCTION

Why do we behave as we do? What makes life worthwhile? Are our actions, our thoughts and our emotions best explained by looking at the biological functioning of our brains? People behave differently and have different personalities. Are these differences best explained in terms of genetic variation? Is our fate in life dictated by our biology? And if that's true, where does this leave free will?

Alternatively, are we corks bobbing along on the tide of events, the unthinking products of social circumstances? We know that people's financial, material and social backgrounds are important. People from different social backgrounds behave differently, and major life events can have traumatic consequences – so are we simply a product of these circumstances? Even if we suggest that we are the result of an interaction between our genes and the environment, that doesn't leave much room for autonomy and free will. It doesn't leave much room for humanity.

Or are we intelligent, enquiring, inquisitive creatures who make active sense of the world? Are we able to understand the world? Can we appreciate the physical environment and the behaviour of other people and form complex, fluid, elegant accounts of the things we see? Are we able to construct mental models of the world?

Although psychology is a relatively young scientific discipline, advances in psychological science over the past few years allow us to understand ourselves with unprecedented clarity. Until recently, the explanations used by psychologists, psychiatrists and neuroscientists have suppressed and compartmentalised human behaviour. Biological accounts have suggested that we are best understood as being the slaves of our brain and, ultimately, our genes. Behavioural psychologists have acknowledged that we learn, and that we are in large part shaped by the events in our lives, but traditional behavioural accounts tend to see human beings as mechanistic robots, shaped by patterns of punishment and reward.

Now, a new approach to psychology – cognitive psychology – is emerging, which offers a much more optimistic vision of the human condition. This approach leads to new ways of thinking – new laws of psychology. It also leads to a fresh approach to mental health – a focus on promoting well-being rather than treating so-called mental illness.

Cognitive psychologists see people making sense of their world, forming mental models, developing complex frameworks of understanding ... and acting accordingly. People are more than the raw products of their biology and are not mere pawns of the vicissitudes of life. People are born as natural learning engines, with highly complex but very receptive brains, ready to understand and then engage with the world. We develop, as a consequence of the events and examples we experience in life, mental models of the world that we then use to guide our thoughts, emotions and behaviours.

These ways of thinking about what it means to be human shouldn't be surprising or strange. In a gentle fashion, this way of thinking could revolutionise our understanding of what it is to be human, of mental health and well-being, even morality and self-awareness. In my opinion, as a clinical psychologist, if we could understand thoughts, emotions and beliefs a little better, we'd understand our mental health in a different way. We would change the way we diagnose so-called 'mental illnesses' and we would offer realistic help to people in distress. These new laws of psychology should change our whole approach to understanding and treating mental illness.

BIOLOGICAL DETERMINISM

Biological explanations of human behaviour suggest that, our behaviour is the product of our brains, and that our brains are the product of our genes. These kinds of explanations were particularly popular in the early part of the twentieth century, and are still commonplace in the media – on TV, the radio, in newspapers. They are seductive. Our brains are clearly responsible for a wide range of important biological functions, and biological explanations for complex human phenomena are common and powerful. The neurotransmitter dopamine (which has been linked to many street drugs and to psychosis) seems to have a role in making events seem more personally significant and salient, and has been linked to a range of mental-health problems, including psychotic experiences such as hallucinations and persecutory delusions. Serotonin (another neurotransmitter) has been linked to mechanisms of reward and social status, and therefore to depression and low self-esteem.

There is a lot of truth in these biological accounts of psychological phenomena. However, biological explanations are not, in themselves, very good at explaining complex behaviours, and they are particularly poor at explaining differences between people, which is usually what we're interested in. At one level, it's obviously true that our behaviour is the product of the functioning of our brains. Every action and every thought we ever have involves the brain. But since every thought necessarily involves the brain, this merely tells us that we think with our brains. This kind of explanation doesn't add much to our understanding. When confident people think about performing in public, their brains are involved in doing the thinking, but that is also true for anxious people – their brains are also involved in doing the thinking. Trying to explain complex human behaviours in neurological terms alone is the equivalent of explaining the origins of the First World War in terms of the mechanisms of high explosives. A simple biological model is difficult to refute but doesn't add much.

A more elegant version of biological explanation focuses on individual differences. This suggests that the obvious differences in behaviour, personality and attitudes are best explained by biological differences between people. In stressful situations, such as natural disasters, some people may experience very significant mental health problems whereas others are strikingly resilient. Biological approaches explain these differences in psychological response to trauma in terms of differences in biological functioning. We might, for example, suggest that some people are likely to experience a significantly greater 'spike' in levels of cortisol – the 'stress hormone'. If you can explain our behaviour in terms of biological processes, it would make sense to intervene with biological solutions. In the case of mental health problems this means medication.

These biological accounts are important and useful. We cannot possibly understand human life in full if we don't understand the working of the human brain. However, these accounts are incomplete. Although a better understanding of the brain is vitally important, neuroscience, without psychology, can explain very little about why two people are different. And many people, myself included, are inherently cautious about intervening biologically – medication is a commonplace response to mental health difficulties but not an attractive one. We have to understand the psychology of how people make sense of their world if we hope to understand human behaviour and emotions, and therefore mental health problems.

SOCIAL DETERMINISM

We are immersed in societies that form, support and mould us. In part, we behave as we do because of the social circumstances in which we find ourselves. Our behaviour is formed as a result of the contingencies of reinforcement to which we are exposed. As we go through life all of us are faced with a myriad of events and opportunities. These tend to shape us and shape our behaviours. Every time we are rewarded for our actions it changes our behaviour. This can be overt reward such as bribery or applause, or the much more subtle but equally effective reinforcement of seeing our parents smile as a result of something we've said, or seeing other people receive rewards for their actions. We are, at least in part, the product of the rewards and punishments that we have received through life. So there is a strong tradition in psychology of using behavioural explanations – accounting for our behaviours, and differences between people, in terms of rewards and punishments.

In the past, many psychologists have been particularly keen on this kind of explanation. Many psychologists have assumed that human behaviour – and even that thinking itself – is merely the product of the pattern of reinforcements and punishments to which we have been exposed. However, as I'll explain in more detail later, these accounts are also inadequate. Although it's true that different experiences in life can lead to different emotional outcomes for people, it's also true that different people respond to and make sense of similar life experiences in different ways. Again, we have to understand the psychology of how people make sense of their world.

THOUGHTS ABOUT SELF, OTHER PEOPLE, THE WORLD, THE FUTURE...

People are more than mere biological machines and are more than unthinking clay, moulded by social and circumstantial pressures. We are more than the biological products of our genes and of the inevitable consequences of contingencies of reinforcement. We make sense of our world.

Our beliefs, emotions and behaviours – including our mental health – are the product of the way we think about ourselves, other people, the world and the future. These thoughts are, in turn, the consequence of our learning: the social circumstances, life events and experiences that we have been exposed to and the ways in which we have understood and responded to them. Our brain is a supremely efficient machine for learning, and we make sense of our experiences.

HUMANITY

Sometimes the most obvious, simplest solution is the best. We can understand people if we understand their life story. Life is complicated. We live in a world that is changing rapidly, both socially and technologically. Politics are global and we are exposed to 24-hour news. Technology is advancing blisteringly fast but in our human lives most things are done for very straightforward reasons – people make sense of their world and act accordingly. We can use this knowledge to understand not only mental health but also other key aspects of our lives – relationships, families, work, happiness, moral decisions. In a world beset by whizz-bang science and advancing technology, this is a call to humanity and simplicity.

MENTAL HEALTH – AND MORE

As a clinical psychologist, I focus particularly on psychological well-being. In this context, the biopsychosocial model of mental health has offered a useful framework for considering the main factors thought to affect our mental health – the biological, the psychological and the social. We know that biological factors affect our mental health. Street drugs (and alcohol, nicotine and caffeine) alter our behaviour and affect our mental health. Genetic factors are associated with mental-health issues, although the relationship is clearly much more complicated than looking for the 'gene for schizophrenia'. Fascinating research in neuroscience has given us important insights into the mechanisms underpinning both commonplace behaviours and mental-health problems. It would be wrong to minimise the relationship between biological factors and human behaviour or mental-health problems, but – and this is a fundamental point – biological factors have their impact on mental health because they affect our psychology.

Social factors are also clearly associated with mental health problems. People from poorer and more socially deprived backgrounds are much more likely to experience mental health problems, and these problems tend to be more serious. Lonely people tend to have more problems than people with close personal confidants. A range of negative life-events are associated with mental health problems – from traumas such as war and civil disasters and personal traumas such as childhood abuse or rape, to more commonplace negative events such as divorce, bereavement or redundancy, and even the cumulative effect of daily hassles. It is very sad, very distressing, but very important to remember that very many of us are survivors of traumatic experiences, including assaults, rape and childhood sexual abuse. Many of us are bullied at school – and in the workplace. These traumas have their impact on our mental health, and change who we are as people. It's unacceptable to suggest that people damaged by their experiences are in some sense inadequate, ill or constitutionally unfit. Again, however, these social factors affect our mental health and emotions because they change how we learn to look at the world.

LEARNING

Although all human behaviour involves the brain, we don't need to look for differences in brain functioning to explain differences between people. The 'job' of the brain is information processing. If two identical twins, with identical brains, had learned to understand the world in different ways, they would behave differently. It's important to understand how people learn to make sense of their world.

Psychological understanding has moved on from the basic biomedical psychiatry of the eighteenth–nineteenth centuries. Some of this psychology has, itself, been simplistic. Early in the previous century, psychologists focused on learned associations – the 'classical conditioning' of Pavlov. This led quite swiftly to the 'law of effect' – the basic principle of behavioural psychology that states that, if an action is followed by a reinforcing, positive consequence, it is *more* likely that it will be repeated, whereas, if an action is followed by a punishing, negative consequence, it is *less* likely that it will be repeated. Obviously, that's important. It has helped shape all kinds of policies and practices, from childcare and education to criminal justice policies.

However, we have moved on further still. Cognitive psychology has established several key facts about everyday human life. Human beings are born as natural learning engines. We have brains that are unique in the animal world, which absorb information at an amazing rate. To develop the adult vocabulary of 20,000 words, children have to be able to learn up to twenty new words a day. This learning is best understood as the development of mental models of the world. These models are complex (and often largely unconscious) constructions that depend on the simultaneous manipulation of abstract representations of the world. To make sense of the world, we have to construct abstract representations of the world such as 'he is trustworthy'. These are abstract because we can't physically touch the 'trustworthiness', but there's very good evidence that our everyday behaviour is influenced by these kinds of representations of the world. It's also clear that most humans have highly complex representations of the world, and are constantly processing information on many levels simultaneously. So, our mental models of the world are built up from the simultaneous manipulation of enormous numbers of complex abstract representations of the world. These models have enormous significance, as they explain how we think, feel and behave – and if you can understand these mental models, you will understand people's behaviour, emotions and beliefs.

This suggests that, although we do differ at birth, differences between people have much more to do with the different experiences and cultures to which we have been exposed. It suggests that biological and genetic factors give us – all – unparalleled learning capacity. This separates us from animals, but explains much less about the differences between people. These differences in behaviour, emotions and thoughts are best explained by differences in our experiences, and the sense we've made of those experiences. This makes neuroscience a servant of psychology, not the other way round.

WE'RE NOT PERFECT

Psychological science tells us that our mental life is largely a constructive process. We build up our picture of the world from the evidence of our senses, rather than 'seeing' an image of the world projected onto our brains. This means that we make a lot of mistakes, and much of our picture of the world is a – very effective – 'best guess'. Research into eyewitness testimony tells us that our memory is fallible. Research into 'change blindness' – the 'invisible gorilla effect' – reveals that people often fail to perceive dramatic changes in their environments, essentially because they are not expecting them.

What we think we see might not always fully reflect the objective reality, and this applies particularly to psychological distress. People become depressed or anxious because of their negative thoughts about themselves, other people, the world and the future. Our frameworks of understanding the world, and especially how we explain key events in our lives, are crucial. Our perceptions of ourselves and the world will be shaped – like all perceptions – by a constructive process. In very distressing cases, people can become deluded and can hallucinate. They can be certain they are being persecuted and that they can hear disembodied voices. However, since we can all make mistakes, these distressing beliefs can be mistaken.

Even our sense of self is a construction. We understand who we are and how we function by making working models of ourselves in our minds – and it's these working models we need to understand. This means that many mental-health problems – paranoia, depression, social anxiety, etc. – may be the result of poor learning experiences rather than biological deficits.

The human brain has an enormous potential for learning. We also – uniquely among all the animals – made a huge evolutionary leap by developing the ability to use abstract concepts. This means that we don't merely understand where things are and make predictions about what might happen next (although we do this too, of course). We also understand what the meaning or implications of these predictions are. We use complex, abstract concepts such as 'trust' or 'love' and manipulate these abstractions. These matter because they have important consequences. Imagine a long-term relationship: the two people would probably say that they love each other and trust each other. If it turns out that one person has been stealing money from their partner on a regular basis, we would expect this to have an impact on the relationship. People behave differently because 'trust' is degraded. Human reasoning is based on the simultaneous processing of multiple abstract representations of the world, and many of our most important behaviours, especially in relation-ships, are shaped in part by these complex and abstract ways of understanding our social world.

Of course, this is fiendishly complicated. So complicated that much of our day-to-day human thought is not based on mathematical logic, but on 'heuristics'. These are simple rules of thumb that permit rapid, if inaccurate, action. People make many (perhaps most) important decisions using precious little logic but instead relying on 'rules of thumb' and rapid, practically useful near-guesses.

THINKING PSYCHOLOGICALLY

All this means that our beliefs, emotions and behaviours – including our mental health – are the product of the way we make sense of the world. Our mental models of the world are constructed using psychological processes that are themselves influenced by biological factors, social factors and life events.

Mental health problems are therefore best understood in human rather than neurological terms. Of course, all mental health problems involve the brain, for the simple reason that every thought we have ever had has involved the neurological functioning of the brain. However, very little of the differences between people in terms of their mental health – or indeed general human behaviour – can be accounted for in terms of variance in neurological processes. Most of the variability in people's problems appears to be explicable in terms of their experience rather than genetic or neurological malfunctions. Reward mechanisms involve serotonin and dopamine ... but that's true for everyone. Neurological accounts are reasonable, detailed descriptions but aren't good explanations. They describe the brain mechanisms involved in a particular behaviour but they don't always explain why those mechanisms are involved.

The explanations developed by behavioural psychologists are also inadequate. It's certainly true that people (and animals) very swiftly learn to recognise which stimuli signal important events in the environment (such as the arrival of food). Equally, we quickly learn the consequences of our actions. Actions that result in rewards tend to be repeated; actions that result in punishment tend not to be repeated. However, while the contingencies of reinforcement are important – and certainly play their part in shaping our behaviour – people are also quick to learn to understand their world in very abstract terms. We learn to predict the future and understand the rules behind schedules of reinforcement. We learn when we are likely to be rewarded and when we are likely to be punished. We learn to understand problems in order to solve them, not merely acting in hope of reward. And we model our behaviour on the behaviour of other people, thus we learn the rules of social behaviour. All this suggests something much more elegant than behavioural psychology has to offer.

WHAT THIS MEANS FOR MENTAL HEALTH CARE

Appreciating the fact that people are actively making sense of the world around them has direct and immediate implications for the practice of diagnosis and the concept of 'abnormality' in mental health. Notions such as 'mental illness' and 'abnormal psychology' come from a medical tradition – assuming that emotional problems can be thought of in the same way as any other illness. However, these ideas are old-fashioned, demeaning and invalid. Diagnostic categories such as 'major depressive disorder' and 'schizophrenia', listed in widely used publications such as the American Psychiatric Association's *Diagnostic and Statistical Manual*, are unhelpful. Indeed, the entire concept of 'mental illness' is relatively meaningless. Millions of people clearly have serious psychological problems. In the UK, suicide is the most common cause of death in women in the year after the birth of their first child and one in four of us will have some form of emotional problem at some point in our lives. The cost to the state from mental ill-health is estimated at billions of pounds per year and antidepressant drugs are among the most common – and most profitable – products of the major multinational pharmaceutical companies. However, ideas of disease or illness are unhelpful and even the concept of 'abnormal' psychology is unreasonable.

Some of the excesses of the diagnostic approach are illustrative. The American Psychiatric Association refers to 'oppositional defiant disorder'— a 'mental disorder' diagnosed in children and characterised by the child being 'wilful' and 'headstrong'. It is not reasonable to differentiate 'normal' from 'abnormal' in this way. It is illogical and unscientific, in that the psychological processes that underpin these emotions, thoughts and behaviours are common to all of us – they do not suddenly appear in people diagnosed with certain 'illnesses'. It is unhelpful, because it creates a divide between 'them' and 'us' and helps to perpetuate stigma. It is much more appropriate to see all these aspects of psychological well-being as lying on a continuum – suggesting that there is no very clear cut-off between normal human distress and 'mental illness'. People are merely making sense of their world, and differences between people are likely to reflect these individually varying frameworks of understanding. If common patterns emerge – if people have common types of anxiety, common modes of thinking – it is good to recognise these. However, developing an understanding of the ways in which people typically make sense of the world cannot simply be equated to diagnosis. It does not, for instance, suggest that there is an underlying illness producing these problems – they emerge from normal psychological processes. It doesn't make assumptions that certain problems will necessarily occur together, nor does it try to distinguish abnormal from normal types of thinking.

Instead, we should remind ourselves that we know a great deal about the key psychological and developmental processes that make us human, and we know how events in our lives, social circumstances and our biological make-up can affect those processes. Addressing well-being from that perspective is both radical and common sense. Scientific research into the psychological processes that we use to understand the world and interact with other people can offer a valid, useful and positive alternative.

The World Health Organization makes it clear that health is more than the absence of illness, and the European Commission has – rather wonderfully – commented that: '... for citizens, mental health is a resource which enables them to realise their intellectual and emotional potential and to find and fulfil their roles in social, school and working life'. For people in distress, the concept of mental illness offers little real benefit. An evidence-based approach to mental well-being – identifying scientific understanding of the key psychological processes that underpin our humanity – instead offers great hope.

So, we could think differently – about the relationship between the brain and the mind, about mental health and so-called mental illnesses, about well-being, about the mental health services and about therapy.

The new laws of psychology recognise that our beliefs, emotions and behaviours – including our mental health – are the product of the way we think about the world, our thoughts about ourselves, other people, the world and the future. These thoughts are, in turn, the product of a process of learning. They are the consequence of our learning. Our experiences, the life events we've encountered, our social circumstances and, importantly, how we have understood and responded to these, have shaped our understanding of the world. Our brain is a supremely efficient engine of learning, and makes sense of our experiences. The resultant framework of understanding or mental model of the world is responsible for our thoughts, beliefs, behaviours and emotions. Differences between people's learning experiences will result in different ways of understanding the world, and hence create differences between people.

Modern, Western, industrialised and medicalised approaches to mental health care are limited. They are based on the 'disease model' — the assumption that emotional problems stem from illnesses that can be diagnosed and treated just like any other physical illness. Psychological principles are applied only rarely and as an afterthought, and when they are applied they are often used in very simplistic ways. We need to move beyond both behavioural and biological explanations of human behaviour to recognising how people actively make sense of the world.

THINKING DIFFERENTLY

Since the 1950s psychologists (and psychiatrists who understand cognitive psychology) have developed a sophisticated and practically useful model of how people understand the world. In straightforward terms, people are born as natural learning engines, with highly complex but very receptive brains, ready to understand and then engage with the world. We develop, as a consequence of the events and examples we experience in life, mental models of the world, which we use to guide our thoughts, emotions and behaviours. These models can efficiently explain a great deal of human behaviour – and the differences between people's frameworks of understanding can explain the differences between people. If you appreciate how people themselves understand their world, their behaviour is largely understandable. These personal models of the world can themselves be efficiently explained by the events and experiences to which a person has been exposed, and offer a more real and fundamental 'cognitive revolution' than the whiz-bang of neuroscience.

If we are wholly the product of our history and the circumstances of our lives, and yet at the same time are entirely the product of the biological functioning of our brains, how can we reconcile this? The fact is that both our brains and our experiences shape our thoughts, but it's our thoughts that count and make us who we are.

This is a positive message because we have the potential to change how we think. An analogy that I occasionally use with clients is to imagine being dropped from a helicopter into the middle of a bog. It's not our fault that we're there but we can – with the right tools and the right help – find our way out of the mire. I'm not suggesting that we can make anything we wish for happen just by imagining it. We can't merely create reality for ourselves through some magical power of pure thought. However, it is the way that we process, interpret or 'think through' the events in our lives that determines how we learn from these events. Our learning history shapes the paths our lives take and therefore our thoughts, emotions and behaviours – our character and personality. We're always learning, and so are able to learn ways to address new challenges in our lives.

THE THREAD OF THE STORY

It's our framework of understanding the world, not our brains and not even the events that happen to us – not nature and not nurture – that determines our thoughts, emotions, behaviours and, therefore, our mental health. There have been fantastic scientific revelations concerning the mechanics of the brain over the past few years. The human brain is amazingly complex, with impressive information-processing power. However, an explanation of human behaviour at the level of the mechanics of the brain is insufficient, alone, to explain the complexities of human emotional life. A little like a high-powered computer, the human brain processes information according to rules, and these rules are learned through our experience and upbringing. People's mental health, well-being and perspectives on the world are all shaped by their environment and the events that have happened to us.

For me, as a practising clinical psychologist, the role of commonplace events in shaping our emotional life is vitally important – and often overlooked. It's very easy to believe that our behaviour is the product of the biological functioning of our brains, and, when people develop psychological or emotional problems, to assume that biomedical explanations and biomedical (drug) treatments are appropriate. However, if you take the time and trouble to understand what's happened to people, their emotional lives, thinking patterns and behaviour usually seem very reasonable. It's by understanding how we go about the complicated process of making sense of the world that we can fully understand our social, emotional and interpersonal lives.

These vitally important mental models of the world have to be learned. We're not born with them (in fact, human beings are born essentially incapable of anything very much – compare a baby human with a baby lamb), but we learn them. We have an amazing capacity to absorb and assimilate information and we manage to develop individual, even idiosyncratic, frameworks to understand the world. This wonderful, fantastic variability in how we make sense of the world determines how we think, feel and behave. It's the software, not the hardware, that matters.

This simple way of thinking about human behaviour has significant implications. All of us want to lead happier, healthier, more rewarding lives. If, in the words of the European Commission, we are to realise our intellectual and emotional potential and to find and fulfil our roles in social situations, school and working life, we need to understand how we make sense of the world. We may need to appraise and reconsider that framework of understanding. Fortunately, it's entirely possible to learn to look at the world differently. And if we change the way we think, we'll change the world.

CHAPTER 1

ARE WE CONTROLLED
BY OUR BRAINS?

The human brain is amazing. Our scientific understanding of the workings of the brain has increased enormously in the past few years, and it's inevitable that this will help all of us to lead longer, healthier, happier lives. It's important to understand the biological functioning of our brains fully to understand human nature, but while it's necessary to understand the way the brain affects our behaviour it isn't sufficient on its own. We cannot explain the complexities of human behaviour merely by explanations at the level of the brain. As with many other complex issues, we need to understand things on many levels, including understanding the brain, neurons and synapses. However, this still isn't enough, because to understand people fully, we need to understand how the brain responds to the environment and the things that happen to us, and we need to understand how we make sense of these experiences.

As a clinical psychologist, I am naturally most interested in our approach to mental health care. It is abundantly clear that our modern mental health care systems are letting people down. In part, this is because we focus too much on the biological functioning of the brain and not enough on how people use their brains to make sense of the world. Making this shift, using modern psychological science, could transform our care of people with mental health problems.

THE MOST COMPLEX OBJECT IN THE KNOWN UNIVERSE

Your brain is routinely described as 'the most complex object in the known universe', at least on the Internet. The human brain is unprepossessing to look at – a pinky-grey wrinkled lump with the consistency of congealed porridge – but appearances are, of course, deceptive. Our brains are amazing because of what they do, not because of what they look like. Every thought, every wish, memory, fantasy or anxiety originates in the brain.

Neurological or biological factors are vital in understanding human behaviour and mental health problems. I've worked as a clinical psychologist for over twenty years and I've struggled alongside distressed people trying to help them turn their lives around. As an academic I've worked hard to make sense of the enormous range of different and, occasionally, contradictory scientific studies of human behaviour and emotions. This has convinced me that we cannot understand the brain's functioning or human behaviour without invoking psychological processes. What is majestic about the brain is the way we use it to process information.

1.8 MILLION NEW CONNECTIONS EVERY SECOND OF OUR LIVES

The brain is divided into two hemispheres, connected by the corpus callosum, with a wrinkled surface of folds (called 'gyri') and clefts (called 'sulci'). These folds give the brain more surface area (which means that more connections between neurones can be supported) and divide the brain up into different regions. Although we have a great deal more to learn about the brain, we know that different kinds of mental activity tend to be represented by activity in different areas of the brain. We've learned that specific regions of the brain have specialised functions by studying the consequences for people who have suffered injury or strokes, and by using more modern imaging techniques. This is a very valuable way to explore the functioning of the brain. As Kenneth Craik put it: 'in any well-made machine one is ignorant of the working of most of the parts – the better they work, the less we are conscious of them ... It is only a fault that draws our attention to the existence of a mechanism at all'.[1] Certainly, as we age, diseases of the brain are hugely important.

However, the fact that studies of the brain's malfunctions and injuries can help us understand its mechanisms shouldn't force us to conclude that these biological malfunctions and injuries are necessarily the right kinds of explanations for all social problems. As well as mental health problems such as depression, crime and antisocial behaviour, personality traits, entrepreneurialism, even political views and religious beliefs have also been explained in terms of biological differences. Other factors are important – almost certainly more important – in shaping these kinds of behaviours.

The two hemispheres of the brain perform different roles. Regions of the left hemisphere are associated with speech and language processes, while the right hemisphere is more important for processing information about physical movement and hand-to-eye coordination (this is true for right-handed people, but the picture is a little more complex for left-handed people). The occipital lobe – a region at the back of the brain – is particularly associated with vision; the parietal lobe (also at the rear of the brain, slightly above the occipital) is associated with movement, position and orientation. On the sides of the brain, just above the ears, are the temporal lobes, which are where information related to sound and, particularly, speech, is processed. The most recognisably 'human' concepts – planning, decision-making and the complex analysis of social relationships – are largely the responsibility of the frontal and prefrontal lobes (the parts of the brain that lie behind the forehead).

Deep within the brain are specialised structures that perform specific roles (see Figure 1.1). The limbic system is involved with memory, smell, appetite, motivation and reward and, in turn, influences the hypothalamus, which is responsible for 'fight or flight' behaviour. The amygdala forms part of a structure called the striatum, and plays a major role in the regulation of emotions, as well as the control of voluntary movement. These structures are important in feedback processes, and are therefore important for learning. Damage to the striatum can lead to Huntington's disease; Parkinson's disease is also associated with this area. The hippocampus is associated with memory formation, the thalamus processes information from sensory nerves, and the hypothalamus (in association with the pituitary gland) regulates a range of bodily processes through the release of hormones. The cingulate cortex deals with our perception of, and reaction to, pain, while the basal ganglia are associated with motivation and reward. At the back of the brain, nestling under the occipital lobes, is the cerebellum. This 'little brain' (the word cerebellum's meaning in Latin) deals with automatic or repeated movements and hand-to-eye coordination. Some neuroscientists believe the cerebellum may also have a role in 'higher level thought' – language, logic, etc. – but this idea is controversial. The midbrain and brainstem – leading down towards the spinal cord – control unconscious processes such as breathing, heart rate, blood pressure and sleep–wake cycles.

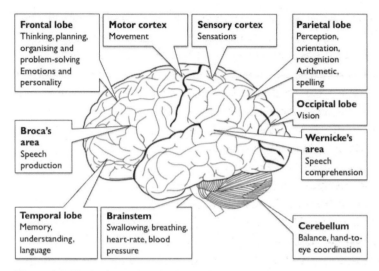

Frontal lobe
Thinking, planning, organising and problem-solving Emotions and personality

Motor cortex
Movement

Sensory cortex
Sensations

Parietal lobe
Perception, orientation, recognition Arithmetic, spelling

Occipital lobe
Vision

Broca's area
Speech production

Wernicke's area
Speech comprehension

Temporal lobe
Memory, understanding, language

Brainstem
Swallowing, breathing, heart-rate, blood pressure

Cerebellum
Balance, hand-to-eye coordination

Figure 1.1 The brain and its principal regions
© Peter Kinderman 2014

With modern computing technology, it's relatively easy to understand how concepts such as orientation, hand-to-eye coordination, or even the maintenance of blood-pressure, require information processing. The brain (quite unconsciously) receives a wide variety of information from what are usefully thought of as 'sensors'. It uses this information and responds by increasing the heart rate, or stimulating the production of various hormones. One of these hormones, of course, is the so-called 'stress hormone', cortisol. Among other things, cortisol controls alertness, and the levels of cortisol in our system vary through the day and across our life-span. This means that we have low levels of cortisol in the early hours of the morning; we don't want to be alert when we're supposed to be asleep. In adults, the level of cortisol rises as we prepare to wake up, but in adolescents, this rise in cortisol starts a bit later. All of which means my fifteen-year-old son is alert late at night, but sluggishly grumpy when he should be getting ready for school.

However, it's not these facts that make the brain complex or indeed interesting. For me, the numbers are impressive, but the implications are stunning. The brain is made of a staggering 86 billion nerve cells or neurons. In addition to the neurons, there are vast numbers – perhaps another 85 billion – of 'glial cells'. These seem to work by magnifying the signals transmitted by the neurons, rather than transmitting information themselves. Glial cells also provide 'life-support' to the neurons. They maintain the temperature, oxygen levels and energy levels of the neurons, clear away dead neurons and provide the insulating myelin sheath that wraps around them. The neurons connect with each other through a branching network of thread-like tendrils or 'dendrites'. Where the neurons connect, they form synapses. When one of the tendrils encounters another neuron, guided by signals we do not yet understand, it can form a connective 'synapse' joining the neurons together. The latter is perhaps a little like a connection in a telephone exchange, and these are the connections that give the brain its complexity. Each of the 86 billion neurons will make connections to tens of thousands of other neurons. When you look at psychology or biology textbooks, the drawings of neurons and their connections look a little like trees, with branches and twigs joining each other at the tips. The official neurological term 'dendrite' is derived from the Greek for tree. In fact, neurons look more like tiny cotton-wool balls; there are so many connections that the cells are furry rather than branch-like (see Figure 1.2).

To try to get an idea of the numbers involved, it would take you 2,666 years if you were to sit down and count each one of the 86 billion neurones, one a second. Each of those neurons is

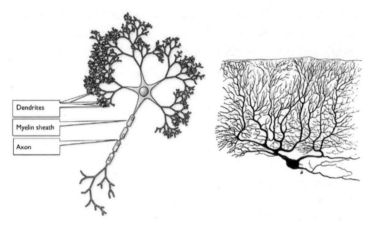

Figure 1.2 On the left, a simplified diagram of a neuron. On the right, a
　　　　　drawing 'from life' of a stained 'Purkinje' neuron from a human
　　　　　cerebellum, illustrating the huge number of branching dendrites
　　　　　(from *Popular Science Monthly*, Vol. 71, 1907; author
　　　　　unknown).

© Peter Kinderman 2014

likely to have 10,000 connections, every one of which affects
our behaviour in a subtly different way... even before the glial
cells assert their influence. Making sense of this incredible
level of complexity isn't easy!

The rate of growth of the human brain is equally staggering.
Although human babies have a great deal of development in
front of them, their brains are already hugely complex, and
it's obviously taken only nine months to get to that stage.
Research conducted on rhesus monkeys suggests that around
40,000 new synapses are created every second (at least until
the second month of life). New synapses are created very
rapidly early in a child's development, but continue to be
made, and broken, throughout life. Some estimates suggest

that we all make 1 million and between 1.8 million new connections every second of our lives. These connections are made, and broken, as a consequence of the stimuli and experiences, the learning we are exposed to over our lifetime. A process called 'neural pruning' means that unnecessary synapses are withdrawn from service. That is part of learning – we 'prune' connections that aren't useful to leave a more straightforward arrangement. This leaves a slightly less complex, but much more useful, network of connections. This, coupled with the fact that neurons die (we don't grow new neurons so it's important to look after the ones we have), means that a three-year-old child has perhaps 50 per cent more synapses than an adult. Our brains, in their hugely complex set of shifting, developing, changing connections, reflect our memories, habits and learning through new physical structures. It is not in the slightest bit surprising that each person's brain is physically different.

NERVOUS ENERGY

The brain is an electro-chemical system. Signals are transmitted down the nerve cells through the rapid movement of charged sodium and potassium ions into and out of the neurons. These movements of charged ions change the electrical potential of the neurons, and are triggered when receptors on the membranes of the neurons detect neurotransmitter and neuromodulator chemicals. There are many of these neurotransmitters: glutamate, dopamine, acetylcholine, noradrenaline, serotonin and endorphins, among others. Most of this chemical transfer occurs in the synapses, but some neurotransmitters affect the functioning of broader regions of the brain. The sequence is intensely complicated, but works something like this: a range of biochemical processes work to maintain a significant difference in the relative concentrations of electrically charged ions (chemical elements) either side of the neurons' cell membrane. This creates a situation in which each of the 86 billion neurons is like a charged capacitor, full of static electricity.

When the receptors on the 'receiving' side of a synapse encounter a molecule of their particular neurotransmitter, the two molecules bond. This triggers a chain reaction within the cell, culminating in the opening of 'channels' in the cell membrane. These 'channels', normally closed, are sprung open, allowing the electrically charged ions to flow through. As these electrically charged ions move in and out of the neuron, it changes the electrical charge of the cell, creating a 'de-polarisation'. It's a little like a static discharge. The consequence of this is that the now-depolarised neuron releases other neurotransmitters from the 'transmitting' side of the many thousand of synapses that it has projected onto other neurons. All of this – the neurotransmitter reception, depolarisation and neurotransmitter-release sequence – is mediated by the activity of glial cells.

It is significant for the action of many psychiatric drugs that biological processes set about returning the neurons to their previous states – mopping up the remnants of neurotransmitters and re-absorbing them into the synapses (where they are stored in 'synaptic vesicles'), and actively moving the electrically charged ions back into the neurons, so that the 'static charge' (technically, the 'action potential') is re-established. This transfer of charged ions does, incidentally, use a great deal of energy; it's been estimated that the brain uses some 20 per cent of our calorie intake – so think more, and lose weight! The rapid depolarisation of neurons, and the consequent spread of electrical activity, transmitted by neurotransmitters across synapses and mediated by glial cells, across the network of the brain, constitutes thought.

Since the brain is the organ with which we think, it's obvious to look within the brain's functioning for the basis of our thoughts ... whether those thoughts concern mental health, happiness or morality.

BIOLOGICAL PSYCHOLOGY

Since every thought must involve activity in the brain, it's very tempting to assume that human behaviour can be explained at the level of the brain. This is an inadequate response, however, for a number of reasons. The idea of 'explaining' things in this way is necessarily difficult. Would you say that a person uses cocaine *because* the drug causes the release of serotonin and dopamine, *because* they have an otherwise unrewarding and unexciting life, *because* they are unconcerned about the possible future consequences of their actions, *because* they are vulnerable to peer pressure, *because* cocaine is readily available and affordable, *because* it's in human nature to seek transcendental experiences, or *because* (as we are occasionally told) some people are inherently criminal? My thoughts do, of course, involve brain activity. If I sit back, close my eyes and think of Eva Marie Saint in Hitchcock's *North by Northwest*, my brain activity will probably change. However, which came first, my thoughts or my brain activity? Which is an adequate explanation of the phenomenon? Since all our thoughts must involve activity in the brain, it's very tempting to assume that problematic human behaviour, such as being quick to anger, should be explained in terms of brain activity. For example, most modern wars involve specific and characteristic movements of the index fingers of men. Does it therefore make sense to explain conflict at the level of the musculature of the human trigger finger?

These apparently esoteric questions have real-world consequences. If those planning and delivering mental health services assume that it is appropriate to explain human behaviour, emotions and thoughts at the level of the biological functioning of the brain, and especially if distress is explained like this, we will see this reflected in the services offered. People will be assumed to have physical abnormalities of the brain, and treated accordingly. This could have dramatic consequences.

There are several examples of this way of thinking – thinking that reduces everything to biology. In 1989, the American psychiatrist Samuel Guze published a short paper entitled 'Biological psychiatry: is there any other kind?'. Guze argued that, since those kinds of behaviours, emotions and thoughts that constituted the subject matter of psychiatry had their origins in the brain, we should look to brain science and biological manipulations of the brain to solve these problems.[2] Eric Kandel softened this rather fundamentalist view a little in a more elegant and informed article in 1998.[3] Kandel's influential article, 'A new intellectual framework for psychiatry' was an attempt to reclaim the biological basis of psychiatry. He proposed a model of mental health – the origins of distress and the most appropriate approach to helping people – that is diametrically opposed to my approach. Kandel argued that organic or biological factors are important in most forms of mental health problems. However, more fundamentally, he also argued that changes in biological functioning (as opposed to psychological functioning) are the 'final common pathway' for mental disorder and, indeed, therapy. So, for Eric Kandel, all the important factors that affect our mental health do so by causing changes in biological functioning. For Kandel, that includes therapy. Kandel argues that therapy works by changing the biology of your brain. For me, all the important factors that affect our mental health (including changes in our biological functioning) lead to changes in how we think about the world, and these then cause problems for some people.

Kandel also argued that any changes in our thinking or behaviour – whether that means learning during childhood, the impact of life experiences or even therapy – reflect physical changes in the neural associative networks. If we make a million new synaptic connections every second, there's certainly support for that view because we don't have any other physical mechanism for learning – the learning has to happen somewhere, and in some way. Kandel also looks at therapy, and argues that any relearning that occurs during therapy is really a biological change in those networks. Therapy, for Kandel, is also a brain event.

On one level, this analysis is obviously true. Any learning must be based on biological changes in the brain at the molecular and synaptic level. However, such an argument is intellectually trivial. All learning – all human behaviour – is dependent on the functioning of the brain, but merely invoking 'the brain' doesn't explain the learning satisfactorily, at least not for me. Of course, a well-functioning brain is necessary for all human activities, but it doesn't really explain why I do one thing in one situation (whereas somebody else behaves differently) or why I behave differently in other situations.

Biological factors must underpin all forms of learning – and therefore each particular learned association. When we learn to be anxious in social situations, there must be a biological process supporting that learning. This makes sense of the million new synapses created every second of our lives.

Learning is making, and pruning (unmaking), connections...
literally, in the case of the brain. So when we learn to associate
a caress with comfort and a sense of security, that learning has
a biological reality in the brain. In exactly the same way,
someone who has survived abuse in childhood may learn to
associate a caress with fear, powerlessness and self-loathing.
Again, this associative learning will necessarily have a basis in
the biological structures of the brain. The fact that there is so
much to learn, every second, means we need a lot of new
connections and a lot of altered connections. However, the
difference between learning to associate a caress with fear, on
the one hand, and contentment, on the other, cannot be best
explained in terms of biological factors. The physical or
biological components of learning – the making of synaptic
connections – don't explain the nature of the learning, they
merely describe how learning works. This is true for all other
psychological processes. The psychological factors important
in mental health problems are no more – and no less – dependent
on neurological processes than are the psychological elements
of normal life: competition, love, honour, guilt, and so on. All
of these are brain-based events.

Other authors – including Guze – have gone even further
than Kandel. They argue that all psychological concepts will
disappear from the psychiatric lexicon as we understand the
neural basis of behaviour because we will have no need for the
notion of psychology. Why stop at the neural level? All brain
events involve biochemistry, and the transfer of sodium (and
other) ions across cell membranes. It is therefore just as
reasonable to say that all learning involves chemistry. By this
analysis, all human behaviour would be complex chemistry,
and therapy would be a chemical event. Or perhaps we could go
further. The chemistry must be dependent on sub-atomic

physics; the processes and the physical forces operating at the molecular level govern biochemical reactions. Is all human behaviour really physics and is therapy a complex phenomenon of electromagnetic forces?

HUMANE APPROACHES TO MENTAL HEALTH CARE

Any research into biological aspects of mental disorder is both welcome and productive. But it is important that such research is properly integrated with psychological and social accounts of the phenomena in question. Many people working in the area of mental health fear that these reductionist, biomedical approaches to mental disorder, the diagnostic systems that are used to classify people's problems, and the explanations that people are given, can lead to forms of care that are both dehumanising and lacking in humanity.

Most biomedical theories of mental health problems and medical treatment suggest that abnormalities in neuro-transmitter functioning are the primary cause of people's problems. Not surprisingly, drug treatments that change the way our synapses work (e.g. selective serotonin reuptake inhibitors) are prescribed. Psychological approaches also involve the brain, but focus on how associative networks (based, of course, on neural processes) help us learn how to navigate our way through life. They rely on theories of learning, perception, appraisal and belief formation, on how we form mental models of the world and how we make sense of our relationships. Psychological models of mental disorder therefore address different sorts of mechanisms than exclusively biomedical theories. They also try to encompass more than the mere mechanics of any individual system and to look at interactions and interrelationships.

THE BRAIN AND THE ENVIRONMENT

As will be discussed later, mental health problems cannot be separated from environmental factors, mainly social issues and life-events. This is as true for psychotic problems as it is for any other. At the same time, there are clear genetic influences here too. Thinking through the relationship between these two, interacting, influences is complex.

One of the best accounts of how the brain and brain systems are implicated in mental health problems comes from the Dutch neuroscientist Jim van Os.[4] Van Os's work focuses on schizophrenia – one of the more distressing forms of psychological distress and in many ways, a quintessential example of a 'mental illness'. He argues that mental health problems, including psychotic experiences such as hallucinations and delusions, should be understood as 'disorders of adaptation to social context'. In other words, this means that people have problems in adjusting to difficult social circumstances. While inherited, genetic, factors are important, environmental factors are also important. He points out that psychotic experiences are associated with a range of environmental factors such as abusive experiences in childhood, growing up in an urban environment, coming from a minority community (such as people in minority ethnic groups), growing up in communities with a larger gap between rich and poor, and the use of cannabis, and concludes that the important pathway leading to psychosis might be exposure to these environmental threats while the brain (especially the 'social brain') is developing. In other words, it's whether or not we are exposed to certain stressful experiences during particular sensitive periods during our development that could determine our mental health – an interaction between genes and the environment.

This way of thinking has important and interesting consequences for our thinking about very serious forms of distress – in the case of psychotic experiences, leading to a diagnosis of schizophrenia, which happens for about 1 per cent of people in their lifetimes. It suggests that these problems might be the consequence of the interaction of stressful life-events (which are, unfortunately, quite common) with a neurocognitive vulnerability that again might be much more common. Jim van Os suggests there might be a common pattern of neurocognitive vulnerability to the effects of a wide range of environmental problems, especially at vulnerable ages, affecting maybe 20 per cent of the population. This is important and interesting because we are no longer talking about a very small number of people (1 per cent) with a specific genetic abnormality, but a much more common (20 per cent of the population) pattern of vulnerability.

Van Os and many other researchers stress that there is clearly a strong genetic element to the underlying 'syndrome', which appears to relate to perception (and therefore hallucinations and delusions), motivation, mood and information processing. Most people now know how we can look at twins to explore the role of heritability. Interestingly, however, there is some evidence that genetic factors seem to be more important (in technical terms, there is a greater level of familial clustering) when people are exposed to those risk factors – such as living in an urban environment or belonging to a minority group. This indicates a strong interaction between genes and environment, but it also means that genes play different roles in different circumstances.

Abusive experiences during childhood are strongly related to future mental health difficulties, and there appears to be a very straightforward 'dose–response' relationship – the more abuse you experience, the more likely you are to have mental health problems later. Although mental health problems in general, and psychosis in particular, can affect people from all backgrounds, being a member of a minority group appears to be a risk factor. This seems, pretty clearly, to be something other than merely concluding that some minority ethnic groups are more at risk than others. The important variable seems to be the 'ethnic density' of the neighbourhood – the more people there are from your particular ethnic group in your locality, the lower your risk of developing mental health problems, particularly psychosis. Van Os (and other researchers) concludes that social adversity, discrimination, social marginalisation and social inferiority are all likely to have marked and profound effects on brain functioning.

Growing up in an urban city environment seems to put people at risk for mental health problems. This is, again, tricky to study, as people move house, so where they live now might not be the same as where they were living when they developed problems. It may also be the case that there are links between different sources of stress – so people living in cities might have more access to drugs, particularly cannabis, and might experience more other negative life events. Life might just be tougher in the city. City living might be associated with greater social fragmentation, with more single parents and less stable households. It does look as if cities present a particular source of stress, and when people move from an urban to a rural environment, this seems to decrease their risk.

Cannabis use has also been widely associated with mental health problems, particularly psychosis. The main component of cannabis, delta-9-tetrahydrocannabinol or THC, obviously affects our thinking and our mood. In higher doses, THC can lead to temporary psychosis-like phenomena, and this effect seems to be greater for people at genetic risk of psychosis – so relatives of people with a diagnosis of schizophrenia seem to be more sensitive to the effects of cannabis. It's a complex link, partly because people tend to use cannabis (as well as many other legal and illegal drugs) as a positive, practical step to help deal with emotional difficulties, and because psychosis might make people more likely to use cannabis. However, it does seem that higher doses of cannabis might make psychosis more likely... at least in vulnerable individuals.

The relationship between genes and environment stretches back before a person is born. A very wide variety of environmental factors that might affect a baby developing in a mother's womb have been suggested as important in leading to adult mental health problems. So maternal stress (which could, of course, affect her hormone levels as well as many other biological factors), maternal nutrition, including vitamin levels, infection by viruses (including influenza and, remarkably, a virus carried by domestic cats), toxoplasmosis and bacteria, and a wide range of complications of pregnancy and birth have all been suggested as important... although it is very rare to find definitive evidence.

Again, all this is important and of interest. A pattern of neurocognitive functioning that has these characteristics – present in one in five of us, and related to perception and emotion – is much more likely to play a positive role in our lives. It is quite likely, for example, that what is being discussed is a tendency to respond more creatively and emotionally to events, and perhaps to see personal significance in events. It is relatively easy to see how this pattern could make one vulnerable to psychosis when also exposed to abusive life events. If people tend to be more fully aware of the personal significance of events (if they mean something to them), tend to feel the consequence emotions a little more, and tend to make connections between events more fully and completely, it is perhaps not too difficult to see how abusive events could trigger a pattern of thought that could spiral out of control. Equally, it could make a lot of sense of why some 'anti-psychotic' drugs can be helpful for some people, and why some street drugs can have negative consequences for vulnerable people.

Many popular street drugs are both desirable and addictive because they tend to enhance this same pattern of thought. Many popular street drugs are reported (by users) to enhance their emotional and creative lives, and to make things more personally salient. When taking these drugs, life seems more vibrant, more colourful, more meaningful, more personally significant. Many drug users warn novices about these effects, and warn that 'bad trips' can occur – when these hyper-salient, hyper-emotional, hyper-perceptual experiences can be overwhelming and negative. On the other hand, many drugs (street drugs as well as medication) tend to make people blasé and 'chilled out' – they are less affected personally by events, slightly dulled and less creative in their thinking, make fewer (rather than more) spurious connections between events, and are generally less troubled by events in their world. This looks very much like an impact on Jim van Os's neurocognitive pattern.

Of course, rather than talking about 'abnormality' we are now really talking about normal psychological processes. It is generally seen as good and useful to be creative, to make connections between events, to see something and make a mental connection to something else. It's generally considered a valuable human trait to feel emotions (especially when the situation objectively justifies such emotions). It's also generally considered good for people to be personally involved with, or engaged in, their social lives. If a person is uncreative, makes no connections between distantly related ideas, is emotionally detached and unperturbed by events, there may well be something wrong. On the other hand, if a person makes spurious connections between unrelated ideas, is emotionally overwhelmed and sees personal salience and relevance in circumstantial events, they may well be at risk from this 'pattern of vulnerability'. What we appear to be looking at is less a 'gene for schizophrenia' or even a 'genetic abnormality', and more the normal variance in human characteristics – with all the positive and negative consequences that naturally follow.

HOW DOES THE ENVIRONMENT SHAPE THE BRAIN?

Serotonin is one of the neurotransmitters responsible for conducting electro-chemical signals across the synapses – from one neuron to another. Serotonin is associated with a range of brain processes (this seems to be a characteristic aspect of brain functioning: since there are many more psychological processes than there are neurotransmitters, each neurotransmitter plays more than one role; the neurons responsible for voluntary movement and perception, for example, both involve dopamine). However, it has reliably been associated with motivation, mood and social status. As a result, abnormalities in serotonin metabolism (the way that neurons use the chemical), and particularly low serotonin levels, are implicated in depression. I mentioned earlier how neurotransmitters are absorbed back into neurons after they have performed their function of transmitting signals across synapses. Many antidepressants (the SSRIs or selective serotonin reuptake inhibitors) work by blocking this reuptake of serotonin, increasing the amount of serotonin in the synaptic cleft (the microscopic space between the neurons). Of course, it's actually much more complex than that, because the brain undergoes other changes when a person takes an antidepressant – for instance, by changing the number, or sensitivity, of receptors on the surface of the neuron.

Importantly, however, we can alter serotonin levels in other ways. Depression responds positively to exercise, perhaps because exercise is effective in raising serotonin levels. In fact, the production of serotonin is increased for some days after exercise, and this appears to be a safer and, probably, better way to increase serotonin levels than the use of antidepressants (especially, of course, because exercise has many other benefits). Serotonin levels can also be controlled by diet. The body manufactures serotonin from an amino acid called tryptophan (both bananas and cheese tend to contain high levels of tryptophan). A diet that is very restricted in tryptophan will lead to low mood and even mild depression because it means there's less serotonin available. In my opinion the most interesting link to serotonin is social status. In studies of animals, dominant male monkeys (the alpha males) appear to have higher levels of serotonin, but when a dominant male loses his elevated social status, these serotonin levels fall. Most interestingly, when a non-dominant (subordinate) male monkey is deliberately given either tryptophan or an antidepressant (both of which will raise the levels of serotonin), they achieve dominant status. In a subsequent, fascinating but disturbing experiment, involving allowing monkeys to administer cocaine to themselves (I didn't design the experiment), it looked very much as if dominant macaque monkeys tended to use less cocaine than subordinate monkeys. Cocaine stimulates dopamine and serotonin release. The researchers believe that the subordinate monkeys may be medicating themselves against their low social status.

The story seems to be that the state we call 'depression' is a natural response to circumstances that involve failure, low social status, abandonment and loss. This state can also result from physical interference with serotonin production. This makes perfect sense, if we assume that the brain – through processes that involve serotonin – is responsible for the information-processing concerning the ways in which people see themselves, their world, and their future. Again echoing the work of Jim van Os, if a person's social circumstances involve prolonged exposure to an environment of failure and loneliness, especially during sensitive developmental periods, there are likely to be longer-term implications for the neurological processes that use serotonin. Again, a biological tryptophan–serotonin system is indeed associated with depression, but there are psychological processes at the centre.

Serotonin appears to be vital to the way that we process information about social status, and intimately associated with mood and therefore depression. It does seem to be the case that life events – both immediately and over a longer period of time – can affect our levels of happiness, our sense of social status and likelihood of receiving a diagnosis of depression. It seems clear, to me, that serotonin is the neurotransmitter involved, but I'm less convinced that the genetics of serotonin is a good way to explain differences between people in terms of their mental health. The neuroscientist Neil Risch and colleagues set out (like many others) to answer this question in relation to depression by examining a large number of previously published research studies examining the role of genetics and life events.[5] They found that people who had experienced more life events were slightly, but statistically significantly, more likely to experience depression. However, they didn't – rather surprisingly – find that the different genes made any difference at all.

THE BRAIN AND THINKING

The phenomena such as hallucinations and delusions that can lead a person to being diagnosed as schizophrenic clearly involve neurological processes. However, it seems clear that these do not simply generate the troubling phenomena, but are also concerned with how we understand our own behaviour and the behaviour of those around us. The intimate relationship between neural and psychological well-being offers intriguing clues to the nature of those processes.

For example, a fascinating story is emerging in the case of auditory hallucinations. There is considerable evidence of a genetic element to schizophrenia, specifically linking auditory hallucinations with cerebral lateralisation. As mentioned earlier, the two hemispheres of the brain are specialised to perform different functions, with language particularly associated with the left hemisphere. The tendency for the brain to perform different functions in the two hemispheres, and therefore to be structurally slightly different, is termed 'cerebral lateralisation'. However, this lateralisation is not absolute, and it looks as if people who hear voices are more likely to have less lateralised (so that is, more even-handed) cerebral hemispheres, and in particular that the brain's language areas are less lateralised in people who hear voices. The tasks of language processing must include working out what sounds are, what they mean and where they come from. The language areas of the brain perform this function, and so any neurodevelopmental issues that affect cerebral lateralisation are likely to contribute to problems in discriminating voices (which are of course heard) from other kinds of thoughts – memories, self-talk, flashbacks, wishes, dreams and so on.

We should not minimise the influence of biological factors in the development of hallucinations, but auditory hallucinations must be understood as psychological phenomena, and emerge from a psychological process. The final, inescapable step to hearing disembodied voices must be the misattribution of internal mental events – you think that you have heard something, but in fact it was a product of your own unconscious brain. This psychological process will be influenced by biological factors, but it is equally influenced by social or environmental factors and the important events in a person's learning history. We know, for instance, that people who have had stressful or abusive experiences tend to be more likely to hear voices.

THE FLOWER OF BRITISH MANHOOD

The trauma of the First World War is part of our cultural history. In his poem 'Mental Cases', the great war poet Wilfred Owen asked: 'Who are these? Why sit they here in twilight? These are men whose minds the Dead have ravished... Pawing us who dealt them war and madness.'[6] Owen knew what he was writing about. He spent the summer of 1917 at Craiglockhart Military Hospital in Scotland after having been evacuated from the front line suffering from 'shell shock'. Many authors, from Sebastian Faulks (in novel form)[7] to Richard Bentall (in academic texts),[8] have discussed the effects of combat on soldiers in the First World War. Part of the story here is that the obvious impact of 'shell shock' on the officer class led to a partial re-thinking about how mental ill-health should be understood. The generally accepted view among the establishment was that the officers, representing selected members of the upper classes, and trained in the education system since youth, represented an example of the human ideal. However, the realities of war were cruel, and a disturbingly large number of young men succumbed to 'shell shock' or combat fatigue, or what those of us who like attaching diagnostic labels to problems would now call 'PTSD' or 'post traumatic stress disorder'. Many were the junior officers – who were expected to lead from the front. Some, of course, were shot as cowards (although, inevitably, those victims tended to be from lower down the social hierarchies). At that point, the most dominant form of explanation of mental health difficulties was biological. More than this, at the time, the eugenics movement was popular. It played its inglorious part in the scientific background of the later rise in fascism and the holocaust. The establishment idolised the noble spirit of the officer class, and generally believed that psychological weakness was biological and constitutional in origin. However, since the 'flower of British manhood' was succumbing to psychological problems, and clearly in response to the overwhelming stress of the horror of the trenches, mental illness could no longer be thought only to lie in inadequate brains and constitutions. There was, clearly, another reason – stress could unbalance the mind.

COMMONPLACE TRAUMA

Psychological distress is common in people who've experienced traumatic events. Refugees and survivors of conflict report high rates of depression and 'PTSD'. Around a quarter of refugees or people who are fleeing conflict either have the problems described as PTSD or report depressed mood. It's sobering that many women report that childbirth is traumatic. We have shared cultural beliefs that the birth of a child is a uniquely happy and positive experience, but for many women, it's a painful, terrifying experience of lack of control. Some secretly fear and regret the birth of their child, and some are physically damaged by the experience. So, it is perhaps unsurprising that many women report traumatic flashback memories of the experience. We'll come back to this point in the next chapter.

More than one woman in ten in the UK has been raped, but only 20 per cent of those women report their assault to the police. Most of the women know their attackers, and an even greater proportion of women – around 50 per cent – have experienced domestic violence from a partner or family member. This violence has major long-term consequences for women's physical and mental health. These assaults are crimes and offences against human rights, but they are also major mental and physical heath issues.[9]

We also damage very many of our children. About one child in every ten is sexually abused in the UK, and about one child in four is physically abused. Many psychologists and psychiatrists have found that abuse is very common in people with mental health problems. These events affect us grievously. In some ways, it's relatively easy to imagine how abuse – especially sexual abuse – could lead to depression and relationship difficulties. It's often tempting to assume that other types of mental health difficulties are attributable to biological causes or the innate constitution of the individual, but abuse is a very common precursor of later serious mental health issues: between 50 per cent and 80 per cent of people experiencing psychotic phenomena report having survived childhood sexual abuse. It's important (unfortunately, because people who are experiencing psychosis might be considered unreliable witnesses) to be clear that around 80 per cent of the reports of childhood sexual abuse can be corroborated by other sources, and people with overt psychotic problems don't appear to be more likely to make incorrect allegations than anybody else. Not everybody experiencing psychosis will have had such a history, but it is widely accepted that childhood abuse is at least one causal element in psychosis.

Paul Bebbington and colleagues recently summarised much of this evidence.[10] People who have survived childhood sexual abuse appear to be about fifteen times more likely to experience psychotic problems. People also experience traumatic events in adulthood. People are bullied, abused, assaulted, robbed and raped. These, too, are associated with major mental health issues, including psychosis. These experiences interact with other factors, including the biological factors discussed in the Introduction. There is some evidence that the combination of childhood sexual abuse and assaults in adulthood is particularly damaging. This combination, coupled with the biological neurocognitive vulnerability mentioned earlier, can be crippling.

DEPRIVATION

We all deal with many stressful events in our lives. The normal and inevitable cycles of birth, childhood, adolescence, success and failure in examination, employment, marriage, moving house, divorce, disease and death affect us all. These major life events are often stressful, even if they are positive – marriage and childbirth are stressful events. It is also important to remember that 'hassles' or ongoing lower-level stress can affect us – overwork, poor housing, financial difficulties, transport problems, relationships problems, etc., and all these pressures are worse if you're poor.

These issues affect children too, of course. Children from low-income families are more likely to show anti-social behaviour, and do less well at school. Poverty is associated with child neglect, and this has predictable impacts on mental health, academic achievement and crime. Accidental and non-accidental injuries in children are more common in poorer families and deprived areas. All of this – to reflect some of the issues discussed in the Introduction – may affect the functioning of the child's developing brain. Stress during childhood may affect what is called the 'hypothalamic–pituitary–adrenal (HPA) axis'. This is a neural system that responds to external threats in ways that include by controlling the release of cortisol, the 'stress hormone' or alertness moderator.

All of these factors have an impact on our mental health, causing leading public health researchers to refer to the 'social determinants' of mental health problems. In the words of a review for the World Health Organization: 'mental disorders occur in persons of all genders, ages, and backgrounds. No group is immune to mental disorders, but the risk is higher among the poor, homeless, the unemployed, persons with low education…' [11] However, it isn't just poverty that's harmful: equality matters, too. In their book *The Spirit Level*, Richard Wilkinson and Kate Pickett outline the evidence that people from unequal countries suffer from higher levels of mental ill-health than do people from countries that are more equitable.[12] Mental health and well-being are clearly socially determined,[13] but there's more to this than pure sociology.

We make sense of the events that shape us. We are not just the product of our genes and brains; nor are we completely explained by the circumstances of our social environment and the events that happen to us. We are not passive sponges as far as these external influences are concerned, because human beings, perhaps uniquely, make sense of the world.

Too much of our language, even the use of the term 'mental health', implies that people in emotional distress have medical or biological problems. Since medical terminology and procedures are used, professionals and the public alike tend to assume incorrectly that people are 'suffering' from 'illnesses', rather than recognising that the problems represent a meaningful human reaction to difficult circumstances. The hugely impressive scientific insights of neuroscience can sometimes be misused. People are damaged by the continued and continuous medicalisation of their natural and normal responses to their experiences. People are often very distressed, and should be helped, but this does not need to be described as 'illness' or 'disorder'. If we regard these experiences as 'disorders', it implies they are abnormal. In what sense is it a 'disorder' if we remain distressed by bereavement after three months or 'pathological' if we are traumatised by the experience of industrialised military conflict?

We need a wholesale revision of the way we think about psychological distress. We should start by acknowledging that such distress is a normal, not abnormal, part of human life – that we humans respond to distressing circumstances by becoming distressed. Any system for identifying, describing and responding to distress should use language and processes that reflect this position.

CHAPTER 2

_____

THE OLD LAWS OF
PSYCHOLOGY

We make sense of the events that shape us. We are not just the product of our genes and brains; nor are we completely explained by the circumstances of our social environment and the events that happen to us. We are not passive sponges for these external influences. Human beings, perhaps uniquely, make sense of the world, but not all psychologists or psychiatrists have seen things in this way. In the past, they have used other theories to explain our behaviour – paying much less attention to our understanding of the world, and instead looking at the physical functioning of the brain, or at the pattern of rewards and punishments to which we've been exposed. Naturally, our understanding of mental health has been shaped, at least in part, by these influential psychological theories. Understanding their strengths and limitations, and how more modern theories have been developed, can help us think in a radically different way about mental health and how to design services.

Psychology is the scientific study of why people behave as they do. In large part, it's the scientific study of why people differ – why they behave differently from one another. There's a relatively well-known experiment involving children and marshmallows. You place a marshmallow in front of a four-year-old child and say: 'I'm going to leave the room now for five minutes. You can eat this marshmallow if you want, but … if, when I come back, it's still here, I'll give you *two*!' Some children can withstand the temptation to eat the marshmallow, but some can't. Apparently, the differences in their performance at the age of four are still detectable many years later – the test seems to be assessing something important. It also seems that the way that children approach the challenge ('how can I resist this temptation?') is important – some sit and stare, and some try to distract themselves.[1] So, why do we differ?

Many different parts of modern society actively apply psychological research. When we discuss bringing up children, education, employment and criminal justice we are discussing psychology and psychological science. Over the past fifty years or so, psychologists have explored how physiological or biological factors influence our behaviour, have introduced the behavioural psychology concepts of 'classical' and then 'operant' conditioning (which I'll explain later), and have studied how people learn by modelling themselves on the behaviour of other people. These behavioural principles have led to Thorndike's 'Law of Effect' – that, if an action is followed by a reinforcing, positive consequence (including the removal of something unpleasant) it is *more* likely that it will be repeated, whereas, if an action is followed by a punishing, negative consequence, it is *less* likely that it will be repeated. Obviously, this is important because it has helped shape all kinds of policies and practices, from childcare and education to criminal justice policies – and stresses the benefits of positive reward rather than negative punishment.

However, I think we have moved on from simple behavioural models. The 'cognitive revolution' of the past twenty-five years has shown us how human beings are born as natural learning engines; that neurology (and the fact that our children are born less fully developed than other animals) has given us unrivalled brains that absorb information at an amazing rate (for example, children's impressive rate of learning new words); and that this learning appears to be best understood as the development of mental models of the world. These models are complex abstract constructions that depend on the simultaneous manipulation of abstract representations of the world. They have enormous significance, because they explain how we think, feel and behave – if you understand these mental models, you can understand people's behaviour, emotions and beliefs.

Cognitive psychology tells us that, although we do differ at birth, differences between people have much more to do with the different experiences and cultures to which they have been exposed, and the way that these experiences have shaped their different understandings of the world, especially the emotionally important aspects of social relationships. Essentially, if you understand what has happened to someone, you'll understand how they see the world. In this view, we are all born with the same basic neural apparatus, with relatively little genetic or biological variance between human beings (although human brains are, clearly, very different from the brains of all other animals). The very different experiences that we have that are, in turn, interpreted differently by each person, make us different. This cognitive, psychological account of human behaviour explains more than a reductionist neurological account. The biological and genetic factors that give us such unparalleled learning engines separate us from animals but don't adequately explain the differences between people. The differences in behaviour, emotions and thoughts seem better explained by differences in our experiences, and the sense we've made of those experiences, than by our brains. Some writers have used the term 'cognitive revolution' to refer to the significant increase in our interest in psychology and neuro-science in recent years. Usually, people focus on the neuroscience aspect, and especially on our increasing ability to take images of the working brain. My focus on the psychological processes represents a slightly different version of the 'cognitive revolution': it considers neuroscience to be the servant of psychology, not the other way round.

BEHAVIOURAL PSYCHOLOGY

Two classic examples of behavioural psychology are Pavlov's salivating dogs and the child having a tantrum at the supermarket. It might not be common, but children do, occasionally, throw themselves to the floor in supermarkets squealing for sweets… and we at least occasionally try to explain this in 'behavioural' terms. Behavioural psychology is essentially about learning, and more specifically 'classical' and 'operant' conditioning (which I'll explain more of in a moment). Learning is, of course, a complex issue, but behavioural psychologists particularly emphasise the role of environmental factors – the things that happen to us – in changing behaviour. Behavioural psychology suggests that we respond to stimuli and reinforcements in the environment, and change our behaviours as a result of what happens to us.

Behavioural psychology, at least traditionally, particularly emphasised the importance of studying observable events – behaviours (and stimuli) – rather than, for example, un-observable thoughts, wishes, beliefs, fears, etc. Behavioural approaches to psychology have been very influential, and many of the key findings are, in my opinion, as close to a definition of 'true' as it's possible to find in psychological science. I feel that an emphasis on science, on hypotheses (rather than clever ideas), on experimentation, on clear operational definitions, and on the measurement of observable behaviours, has been valuable. I also believe that many explanations based on principles of behavioural psychology seem plausible, and behavioural approaches are powerful tools for clinical psychologists and other psychological therapists.

CLASSICAL CONDITIONING: PAVLOV'S DOGS

Ivan Pavlov was a Russian physiologist, studying biological processes of digestion in the last few years of the nineteenth century. Pavlov wanted to examine the rate at which the dogs produced saliva, and so he inserted tubes into their salivary ducts and then introduced powdered meat into their mouths (see Figure 2.1). Pavlov noticed that the dogs tended to begin salivating before the food was placed in their mouths – this was strange, because Pavlov's natural assumption was that the saliva was produced as part of the digestive process, which he thought would begin when the food entered the mouth. Pavlov's dogs, however, began to salivate before the powdered meat was put into their mouths, and then as soon as the person feeding them entered the room. Pavlov's subsequent research into the phenomenon led to the study of what we would now call 'classical conditioning'. For example, Pavlov used a bell to announce feeding time to his dogs, and found that the dogs started to salivate in response to the bell.[2]

Classical conditioning is complex, but is a fundamental part of life. We learn to avoid pain, poisoning, etc. through the mechanisms of behavioural psychology. Typically, for psychologists at least, the classical conditioning process involves

Figure 2.1 Ivan Pavlov and one of his dogs

pairing an event that normally, naturally, leads to a response (for Pavlov, the powdered meat, leading naturally to salivation) with a new stimulus (the bell). If the two stimuli (the bell and the real food) are presented together, then some form of association occurs, and the person or animal now responds to the new stimulus (the bell) with the same response that it originally gave to the food.

On the face of it, this form of learning is pretty simple – the food used to make the dogs salivate, the food is paired with a bell, so now the bell makes the dog salivate. Professional psychologists, of course, look at all the complexities. It's a matter of some debate whether the person (or dog) is now responding to the bell 'as if it's the food', or whether the bell 'makes the person (or dog) think of the food', or whether this is some kind of automatic response, with the bell 'triggering the food response'. These kinds of debate are (at least for psychologists) more interesting than they appear, because they raise almost philosophical discussions about how our thoughts work. Psychologists, of course, have studied all the complicated different ways in which conditioning works, which includes how people 'un-learn' associations as well as how they learn them.

Classical conditioning does have practical, clinical applications. There are a few behavioural therapies that rely on the principles of classical conditioning. People with a range of anxieties can benefit from using the principles of classical conditioning – in this case to break down learned associations, for example, therapists might use a helpful approach called 'graded exposure'.

In graded exposure, the therapist and client draw up a list of anxiety-provoking situations, and then steadily work through that list – hierarchically. Starting with the least anxiety-provoking, the client is encouraged to remain relaxed, and then move steadily up the list until they can remain relaxed even in the face of a situation that earlier had made them extremely anxious. Graded exposure is very effective. Classical conditioning is a powerful process of learning, especially the learning of fear and avoidance, and the detailed psychological studies into how people learn to break, as well as make, associations can offer real help.

REINFORCEMENT

Classical conditioning is not, however, the best way with which to explain the child having a tantrum at the supermarket and throwing herself squealing to the floor at the till. The explanations for why people behave as they do also involve another branch of behavioural psychology – operant conditioning (it's called 'operant' conditioning because it refers to the fact that the person or animal 'operates' on the environment, and in the case of a rat, operates little levers). So, while *classical* conditioning applies to reflex or involuntary behaviours, *operant* conditioning, associated with psychologists such as B.F. Skinner and E.L. Thorndike, refers to the way in which we respond to the environment – we learn as the result of the consequences of our actions.

The explanation for the child's tantrum in the supermarket (to come to the point) is that the child has learned, from previous experience, that she will be rewarded for her tantrums. The classical explanation is that, in the past, when she's moaned or complained, her mother or father has 'given in' and rewarded her with a chocolate bar. That's clearly a positive thing, and acts as a reward … for complaining. The next time they go to the supermarket, the child is a little more likely to complain (she's been rewarded for it in the past) and so has a little moan. It's quite likely that the father won't want to give her chocolate bars every time she misbehaves, so it might take a little more than a suggestion … and over time, with rewards being given when the behaviour is just annoying or embarrassing enough that the father thinks it's the lesser of two evils, the behaviour is developed into fully fledged tantrums.

Perhaps the classical idea of operant conditioning is the rat in the 'Skinner Box' – a kind of experimental cage named after the American psychologist B.F. Skinner. In the box is a lever (it's usually a little aluminium shelf) and devices for flashing lights or buzzers (see Figure 2.2). When the light comes on, the rat presses the lever and a pellet of food drops down. There are of course many variants of this system, but generally the point is that whatever it is that enables you to get the reward tends to be what you learn to do.[3]

Figure 2.2 A rat in a 'Skinner Box'
© Peter Kinderman 2014

Psychologists tend to use the slightly more technical term 'reinforcement'. This refers to anything that, applied after a specific behaviour, increases the probability that the behaviour is repeated. The obvious everyday example would be giving treats to dogs to persuade them to behave on command. If you reward your dog with a little treat each time he sits down when you say 'sit' (you might need to push his back legs down the first time … but it's a sign of how powerful operant conditioning is that he'll soon get the hang of it), he'll very swiftly learn that sitting on command will guarantee rewards. It's notable, incidentally, that some more highly trained dogs – such as the dogs that seek out explosives and drugs at airports – are rewarded by playing games with their handlers, not with food. However, in any case, the dog treats are reinforcers because, if they are given after the dog sits to command, that will increase the probability of his sitting when instructed to do so.

Reinforcement is important in everyday life. We praise and reward people every day. We praise our children (I hope) for their positive behaviour, praise our employees (perhaps less often than we should) for their contributions ... across our private and working lives: we reward people for their behaviours in the hope that this will increase the probability that the same behaviour will be repeated. Psychologists suggest it's useful to think about four types of reinforcement: positive reinforcement, negative reinforcement, and two types of punishment.

The most obvious examples of reinforcement are usually rewards – *positive reinforcement*. The rat receiving a pellet of food, the dog receiving a treat, the child receiving a word of praise and me receiving my salary cheque are all examples of positive reinforcement. I do something and, as a consequence, something positive happens, and that makes it more likely that I'll do it again.

Negative reinforcement also increases the likelihood of a behaviour being repeated. This can also be thought of as escape. Negative reinforcement occurs when an unpleasant stimulus is removed following a particular behaviour, which is appealing, and this reinforces the behaviour. The best example I can think of is when we go shopping and experience very loud, poor-quality music over the tannoy system. If you actually ask the shop manager to turn it down, the blissful pleasure you'll experience at not having your ear-drums assaulted will be a reinforcer for your courage in making the request.

In addition to two types of reinforcement (both of which make behaviours more likely), there are two forms of punishment (which make behaviours less likely). The most ordinary sort of punishment occurs when something unpleasant happens as a result of a particular behaviour. In psychology experiments, people may be given mild electric shocks or a loud noise. In the criminal justice system, punishments (aimed at reducing the likelihood that people will repeat their behaviour) are of course ubiquitous. In everyday life, punishments occur all the time – we bite into apples and are punished by eating maggots; we shout at our children; we rub sunscreen onto our heads without thinking first; and scrape sand all over our sunburn … there are endless examples. In addition, we can reduce the likelihood of a behaviour being repeated if something positive is withdrawn as a result. The classic example would be 'grounding' a child for misbehaviour – nothing actually bad is given as a punishment, but, as a result of their actions, the child isn't able to benefit from all the opportunities for positive enjoyment. The point is the same: a particular behaviour is less likely to happen again either because it leads to bad things happening or good things not happening.

Psychological research is clear that positive reinforcement is generally much more effective in changing behaviour than any of the other options. It's true that punishment (active punishment) is often quite effective in reducing the likelihood that a particular behaviour is repeated, but punishment seems to have a relatively short life-span. Punishment also tends to result (in humans) in emotional states such as anger, and this can often have negative consequences, but, perhaps most importantly, punishment doesn't (by definition) help a person learn what they *should* do. It merely helps a person learn what *not* to do, and it reduces the likelihood that a target behaviour is repeated. In practical, human terms, it means that someone fined for a minor criminal offence may resolve to 'go straight' immediately after conviction, but that resolve tends to fade, perhaps partly because the fine (of course) doesn't teach them any useful life skills.

There are several important details in which reinforcement can change our behaviour. In particular, we can alter the way in which we organise the relationship between the behaviours and the consequences. It's relatively rare, either in experiments or in nature, for a specific consequence to follow each and every time a particular behaviour occurs. The consistency of response is important in the case of punishment, as inconsistency in applying punishments tends to lead to poor outcomes. In the case of positive reinforcement, rewards can be offered each and every time a behaviour occurs, although this is clearly difficult to sustain. It's also the case that, once such a regime is started, if a reward is then missed, the behaviour tends to fall off swiftly. In the case of a rat in a 'Skinner Box', or people in real life, rewards can be offered on a 'fixed ratio' – so you get a reward after every third (or seventh or thirty-third or whatever) time you perform the target behaviour. A variant of these schedules is very popular in casinos – slot machines tend to be programmed so that they pay out (on average) on one in three plays. The major benefit – for the casino managers – is that the casino customers' behaviours tend, then, to be very powerfully reinforced. The pattern is not exactly predictable, but sets up the general expectation that rewards can be expected if you persist, which means that people tend to carry on putting money in even when they haven't received much in return. A slightly different approach to reinforcement is to arrange it so that you're rewarded for the first incidence of a particular behaviour after a certain time period has elapsed. This tends, of course, to mean that people (if you apply this schedule to humans) will swiftly learn to behave in the 'right' way when the time is right – being nice to your parents just before your birthday, perhaps.

The behavioural phenomenon I like most is called 'Premack's Principle', after David Premack. He suggested that behaviours themselves can also be rewarding, and some behaviours or activities are inherently more rewarding, more reinforcing, than others. So eating chocolate is a little more rewarding than writing book chapters. Premack's Principle states that the more desirable behaviour can act as a reinforcer for the less desirable behaviour. Or, in other words, if you make eating chocolate contingent upon writing a book chapter – I won't have any chocolate until I've finished this chapter – then the frequency of chocolate-eating goes down, and the likelihood of writing goes up. All of these complicated processes of applying reinforcement are meat and drink to behavioural psychologists, and have been summed up in what is called the 'Law of Effect', credited to E.L Thorndike. The Law of Effect is one of the very few scientific 'laws' used in psychology, and states that: behaviours that result in a positive outcome are more likely to be repeated, whereas behaviours that result in a negative outcome are less likely to be repeated. It's a simple rule, but one that affects a very great deal of human (and animal) behaviour. In practical terms, it's an enormously powerful tool for trainers.

A few years ago in the UK there was a TV beer commercial featuring a squirrel. To the accompaniment of the theme from *Mission: Impossible*, the squirrel shimmied up a pole, crossed a sciurine tightrope, scurried through a tunnel and leaped over a gap, wobbled across a teeter-board and jumped another gap, ran across another tightrope, ran through a couple of tiny cat-flaps, climbed a rope, and scurried up a plastic tube before leaping across a final huge gap. A good advert, but also a perfect example of an operant conditioning technique called 'shaping'. In order to get to the nuts (the final goal), which acted as reinforcers, the squirrel will have been rewarded for leaping across ever-wider gaps in real life. After mastering that – or, more technically, after consistently responding to the expectation of reinforcement – the squirrel will have been required to climb a short rope before making the leap, then a slightly longer rope ... and the complex pattern of behaviours built up progressively.

Behavioural accounts of human behaviour are compelling because so much of our behaviour does seem to be influenced by the contingencies of reinforcement that apply in the world. B.F. Skinner was, perhaps, the most confident and well-known behavioural psychologist. He, as well as inventing the 'Skinner Box', extended the principles of operant conditioning rather widely by publishing a novel – *Walden Two* – in which he imagined a utopian world based almost entirely on behavioural principles.[4] He also suggested – entirely logically for a behavioural psychologist – that language was developed through operant conditioning. Essentially, Skinner believed that reinforcement as a result of contingencies of rewards and punishments for vocalisations shaped young children into appropriate use of language. However, this radical approach to behaviouralism was very strongly opposed by other psychologists.

On the face of it, behavioural approaches to psychology seem powerful. Even if we leave to one side Skinner's assertion that language was developed through operant conditioning, there seems to be a great deal of sense in the idea that a large proportion of human behaviour is a product of these processes of behavioural learning. If the extreme biological deterministic view of human behaviour could be summarised as 'human behaviour is the consequence of our biochemistry, the anatomy of our brains and the biological functioning of our brains', the extreme behavioural view could be expressed as 'human behaviour is the consequence of the contingencies of reinforcement to which we've been exposed'.

So is that it? Is humanity and the rich complexity of our emotional lives nothing more than the consequence of behavioural principles? Well … it might be more complicated than that.

THE ROLE OF THOUGHTS

In 1974 William Brewer published a well-regarded academic paper with the title 'There is no convincing evidence for operand or classical conditioning in adult humans'. (This perhaps seems a slightly mundane title for most people, but it was designed to annoy a lot of psychologists.) Brewer wasn't really arguing that Thorndike's 'law of effect' wasn't true, because he knew that events that are followed by positive consequences are more likely to be repeated, whereas events that are followed by negative consequences are less likely to be repeated. Brewer's point was that these phenomena require thought, and don't depend on purely behavioural principles.

I hinted at this earlier. It's reasonably well established that casino slot-machines encourage keep people gambling because they are set up to pay out on a variable-ratio reinforcement schedule. This means that, if you put a coin into a slot-machine and it fails to pay out, you're still quite likely to put another coin in, but if you go to a vending machine – for a can of Coke, for instance – put your money in and nothing comes out, you certainly wouldn't repeat the exercise. The point is a simple and obvious one – you understand the difference between slot-machines and vending machines. You don't merely need repeated experiences of variable-ratio and fixed-ratio devices, but you need to have an understanding of what's going on.

Very early in the history of psychology, before the rise in popularity of behavioural approaches, a German psychologist called Wolfgang Kohler was observing chimpanzees. As part of his research, he gave them a range of objects to play with, such

in the same room, with the same toys. In one case, these adults completely ignored the Bobo doll. In the other group, the adults were unambiguously aggressive towards the Bobo doll – punching it and hitting it with a toy mallet. The question was, without any form of reinforcement, what would the children do? Not surprisingly, Bandura and his colleagues found that those children who had seen an adult behaving aggressively were themselves more likely to behave aggressively.[6]

Psychologists studying social learning theory have suggested that people can observe others modelling behaviours – with the result that they are more likely to behave in a similar manner. However, they can also, of course, respond to verbal instructions – we can ask (or tell) a person to behave in a particular way. There's also 'symbolic learning', where people learn from the media, films, television, the radio, the internet, books, newspapers and magazines. This phenomenon is unsurprising to most people; it involves the well-known concept of a 'role model', but it does pose a threat to a simplistic behavioural approach. These children haven't been rewarded; their behaviour hasn't been reinforced. It is obvious that the actions of other people influence our own. This kind of phenomenon is ubiquitous. In fact, it could be argued that a large proportion of our behaviour is learned in this fashion – effectively by learning from others.

MENTAL MAPS ...

Different people react in different ways to the same event. This is important in understanding why some people become depressed or anxious when other people are unaffected. What might seem trivial to you might be very personally significant and very depressing for me. In other words, the emotional importance of an event is a personal issue, not an objective fact. Sometimes people can experience mental health problems following a series of events that we can recognise as obviously depressing (people might lose their jobs, experience a marriage breakdown, suffer a devastating loss). On the other hand, it's occasionally tempting to believe that some people appear to become depressed without there being an obvious external event, but it's rather dangerous to accept this at face value. We don't know why particular, apparently trivial, events are significant for anyone else. As we make sense of the experiences we have through our lives, we develop particular and distinctive frameworks of understanding. These can have understandable but unfortunate consequences, for instance, if a person is bullied at school and learns to accept the negative views of other people. We tend to interpret things very rapidly, in line with our prior expectations. And this can lead us to jump to the wrong conclusions.

At the most fundamental level, people clearly don't record events and images like a video-recorder does. Instead, our brains (and indeed wider nervous system – some basic image-processing happens in the neurons of the retina itself) construct a representation of the world. It's difficult to think of a perfect analogy of what's in our brains in this respect – it's a bit like an interactive, animated, storyboard of a cartoon movie. It's not a photographic duplicate of the world; it's more like an artistic representation of the world as it appears to be. We see the world in unique, individual ways, and each of us sees the world in a particular style, from a particular perspective, and to serve a particular purpose. Those styles, perspectives and purposes are changing from moment to moment. We tend to see what we're expecting and not see what we're not expecting. We even tend to see what we want to see …

That means that sometimes we don't see things – obvious things – even though they are there. Perhaps the best-known example of this is the 'invisible gorilla' – as described in the book of the same name by Christopher Chabris and Daniel Simons.[7] The basic set-up involves participants in a psychology experiment being told that they are taking part in a test of 'selective attention', and asked to watch a video of a group of six university students playing with basketballs. Three people are wearing white shirts, and three wearing black. They are asked to count the number of times the players in white pass the ball. The players move around a lot, ducking past each other in a complex ballet. At the end of the movie, instead of being asked how many times the ball has been passed, they are asked … 'so, did you see the gorilla?' That could have spoiled the presentation (which you can see on their website), but I think the title of their book gave it away too. While the players are passing the ball and dodging in and out, a character in a comedy gorilla-suit walks into the scene, thumps its chest gorilla-style and walks off stage. It spends nine seconds in total on the screen – and is entirely incongruous. However, surprisingly, about half the people taking part in this experiment simply fail to report the gorilla. As Chabris and Simons say, 'it was as though the gorilla was invisible'.

MAKING SENSE OF THE WORLD – AND MAKING MISTAKES

The world is not projected in photo-realistic detail onto our brains. Instead, we are constantly making active mental representations of the world, which occur everywhere. What we see – or think we see – is a mental representation of the world. We miss things and 'see' things that aren't there. This is illustrated experimentally when people fail to see gorillas, but we know the phenomenon is more general – we often see things that aren't there as our minds try to create the most useful (which may not always be the most strictly accurate) picture of the world. More generally, we miss a very great deal, and our minds fill in the gaps.

SOMETIMES WE CAN'T TRUST OUR OWN SENSES – AUDITORY HALLUCINATIONS

Hearing voices – auditory hallucinations – is one of the more iconic phenomena of madness. As I'll explain later, all kinds of mental health problems lie on continua, and many people have unusual experiences in which they think they've heard disembodied voices without anything untoward happening, and without the experiences meaning, or leading to, anything else more serious. It's also clear that hallucinations can be very distressing experiences: at their most innocuous, many people will half hear, half imagine snatches of music, or think they've heard the door-bell ring while they're doing the hoovering. At their most extreme, some people can be plagued by the voice of the devil – as real as if a person were standing in front of them – telling them that they are going to hell. These voices can, for some unfortunate people, continue all day, can be as loud as normal speech or even shouting, and can involve the most appallingly distressing things.

Auditory hallucinations are closely associated with the diagnosis of 'schizophrenia'. Up to 75 per cent of people receiving a diagnosis of schizophrenia report auditory hallucinations, and it's possible to receive the diagnosis of 'schizophrenia' as a result of reporting hearing voices alone, with no other symptoms. However, is it also clear that auditory hallucinations are a much more common, and more 'normal', phenomenon. First, people with problems such as depression also occasionally experience hallucinations, and hallucinations are quite common following bereavement, with people frequently hearing or even seeing recently deceased loved ones. Hallucinations are also relatively common following traumatic experiences, but more importantly, reasonably large numbers of the general population experience hallucinations – at least occasionally. Somewhere between one person in a hundred to one person in every three has experienced occasional, brief hallucination-like events, such as hearing one's own thoughts. What seems to separate people who seek help from the larger majority is whether or not the experiences are distressing.

The best psychological explanation of auditory hallucinations is that people are mistaking their own internal, private thoughts for external events. More precisely, there is compelling evidence that hallucinations are misattributed inner speech. Inner speech or sub-vocalisation is extremely common, accompanying nearly all mental activities that involve active thought or use autobiographical memory. People use inner speech – or actually mutter to themselves – when busy with complex tasks, although they may not always be aware that they are doing so. As early as 1948, researchers found that there was measurable muscular activity of the lips and tongue when people were hallucinating, and modern high-tech methods (such as electroencephalography [EEG] or single-photon emission computed tomography [SPET]) have shown that auditory hallucinations are accompanied by activity in those areas of the brain associated with language production and comprehension. However, although this is very important it isn't the full story. Most of us mutter to ourselves under our breath, but most of us don't experience hallucinations. Cognitive psychology suggests that many of us regularly see things, hear things and believe things that aren't there and aren't true. In the case of hallucinations, it seems clear that people hear voices when they mistakenly 'hear' their own thoughts or sub-vocalisations as voices, and, because they fail to recognise them as their own, they naturally hear them as somebody else's. We need to know why and how this happens. Of course, cognitive psychology helps ... and helps to de-stigmatise this phenomenon. We're not looking at the aetiology of a mental illness, rather we're exploring why people make mistakes – just like the mistakes of change blindness (the invisible gorilla) or eye-witness testimony.

We construct models of the world all of the time, but psychological experiments into phenomena such as change blindness and eye-witness testimony show us that the sense we make of the world is frequently imperfect. We see things that aren't there, and we fail to see things that are. We hear things that aren't said, and we miss things that were. Hallucinations are the consequences of how our perceptual system works. As we struggle to piece together a coherent sense of the world, we construct a mental picture of what's happening. One vital part of this picture, in the case of auditory hallucinations, is the determination of whether something heard is an external voice or the person's own thoughts. Psychologists talk about the 'cocktail party' phenomenon – the fact that we are able to pick out somebody saying our name across a crowded room with many overlapping voices and noises. So, somewhere in the brain, we have a system for working out who said what, and the evidence is clear that this system also has the job of filtering out thoughts from voices. It works in the same way as any other psychological system: we construct a picture of reality. It might be supposed that the neural pathways for 'thought' should be entirely separate from the neural pathways for 'a voice I've heard', but that simply isn't the way our brains are built. We use the parts of the brain responsible for generating speech and language in both of these complex jobs, so it's easy to make mistakes. It's easy to think that you've heard something you haven't, and this becomes more likely if you are naturally prone to those sorts of errors: if you're very stressed, if you're already generating the kinds of intrusive, automatic, negative thoughts that are easy to misinterpret, if you've had traumatic experiences, or if you worry about keeping control of your own thoughts.

So it's not at all surprising that sometimes people hear voices. These kinds of ways of understanding psychological processes can lead to very effective psychological therapies – including for hallucinations – which are very effective. These will be discussed in later chapters.

THE NEGATIVE COGNITIVE TRIAD – YOU CAN BE WRONG ABOUT BELIEFS, TOO

One of the more important advances in a psychological under-standing of mental health problems was made by a psychiatrist. In 1979 the Philadelphia-based psychiatrist Aaron T. Beck, along with colleagues, published a book popularising a very effective way of thinking about, and treating, depression.[8] Beck explains how depression can best be thought of as a normal, although obviously distressing, 'mode' of thinking. He suggests that the emotions, behaviour and physiological status associated with profound sadness, weariness and negativity stem from the way we make sense of the world. As with all mental health problems, depression lies on a continuum from normality through to serious and potentially life-threatening misery. Depression is very common. It has been called the 'common cold' of psychiatry, and is the most prevalent reason why one in four of us will experience mental health problems at some point in our lives. Winston Churchill experienced repeated episodes of depression throughout his life, which he called his 'black dog'.

All of us experience some depressive problems – when a relationship ends, when we fail an important exam or when we make a mistake at work. For most of us, this doesn't last for long, and usually doesn't have major negative consequences, but for some people it's much worse. When depression becomes serious – when it's serious enough to merit a diagnosis or require help from mental health services – it is characterised by persistent low mood, or 'anhedonia', an inability to enjoy things that would normally give pleasure, weight loss or gain, sleep problems, a loss of energy or lethargy, and recurrent thoughts of death or suicide.

Depression has been subject to the same analyses as all other psychological issues and mental health problems and, as with all other problems, depression has also been explained as a product of our genes, an inevitable consequence of our social circumstances, and as the result of the contingencies of reinforcement to which we've been exposed. Beck, however, explains depression in a way that I find much more convincing. He – and I – believe depression primarily to be a consequence of the way we think.

In the 1960s, several psychologists and psychiatrists had begun to realise that cognitive psychology could be applied to mental health problems. Aaron Beck took this cognitive, psycho-logical analysis of depression – and others – but developed, elaborated, and popularised it. He developed much of the intellectual basis of the current popularity of cognitive behavioural therapy, CBT. Beck's cognitive model of depression is soundly based on the idea that people make sense of their world as a result of the things that happen to them in life, and this affects their mental health.[9] Beck suggested that in our early childhood we develop personal 'schemas' – frameworks for understanding the world, especially our social relationships. He suggested that the events that happen to us and all the factors that affect our emotional development – especially parenting styles – give us our unique outlook on life. Beck suggested that, in the case of mental health issues such as depression, these could be thought of as 'dysfunctional cognitive schemas', and it's these that lead to depression when triggered by negative life events.

In Beck's cognitive model of depression, low mood is inevitably accompanied by negative automatic thoughts, which occur spontaneously, without conscious deliberation. In people suffering from chronic depression, they can become reflex or habitual. Although there are obvious themes (negative automatic thoughts in depression often concern failure, worthlessness and loss, in anxiety they concern threat and risk, in eating disorders they concern control and food, etc.), they are usually very personal and specific, and relate to a person's particular situation or experience. As the name suggests, negative automatic thoughts are repetitive, obsessive, involuntary and hard to 'turn off'. For the depressed person, they usually appear plausible and reasonable – even obvious and irrefutable. There are a few final points, important in the cognitive model of depression. These thoughts will naturally lead to the emotional and behavioural elements of depression without the depressed person being particularly aware that they are having these thoughts. They stem logically from the person's belief system or 'schema'. They are the consequence of the inevitable human tendency to construct a mental model of the world – and to piece together the pieces of the jigsaw – and, most importantly, they can be wrong. We all make mistakes (think of change blindness and eye-witness testimony), and many of our thoughts may well be mistaken.

So depressed people have negative automatic thoughts such as 'I'm worthless, there's nothing good about me', 'life is hopeless and pointless, I may as well give up', 'nobody loves me, I'm just a burden on everyone', 'whatever I do will turn out wrong', 'I'm an inadequate parent' or 'getting depressed is a sign of weakness'. If a person's problems are mainly anxiety-related, their negative automatic thoughts might be 'what if I lose control or make a fool of myself, and people think I'm weird?', 'I won't be able to cope on my own', 'what if I get lost?', 'if I make a mistake, something bad might happen' or 'what if this is cancer?'. Taking a lead from the emerging science of cognitive psychology, Beck also suggested that these negative automatic thoughts emerge as a result of distortions, mistakes or errors in the thinking processes of depressed individuals. The negative automatic thoughts are what the person is thinking; the distortions in thinking are how the person is weighing up or judging the information in front of them. Beck identified several common errors, such as 'all or nothing' thinking, where a person sees things in black or white, either/or categories. This can lead to problems; for instance, in the example above, if I were to think in such categorical terms about success or failure, a 'B' grade might lead to depression – since I didn't get an 'A', and everything less than success is a failure, then a 'B' is a failure ... and, if any failure is due to my stupidity... a 'B' means I'm stupid. Other thinking errors, in Beck's model, include overgeneralisation, where a single example is seen as evidence of a more widespread pattern (a single failure is evidence that ' I always screw everything up'). People prone to depression may minimise the positive aspects of a situation and maximise the negative – the classic 'glass half-empty versus glass half-full' position. People jump to conclusions (and, if depressed, to depressive ones), and make assumptions about what is happening in other people's minds. Catastrophising – expecting and predicting the worst possible outcome – is common, as is what is called 'emotional reasoning', which is assuming that the fact that you feel bad (depressed or anxious) is evidence that the situation actually is bad.

PARANOIA ... AND SOMETIMES THEY ARE OUT TO GET YOU

The subtleties of the kinds of explanations we choose are very important. My PhD, under the supervision of Richard Bentall, focused on paranoid delusions. We were looking into why people might end up believing that others are plotting to hurt them. This has been a project for Richard for many years, and – as with all these problems – there remain many questions to answer. In general, however, the same principles apply to paranoia as depression, anxiety and other problems; that is, people are constructing a mental representation of the world, piecing together scraps of information to try to understand the events around them. Sometimes, people make mistakes, and gradually begin to believe that they are in serious danger. I remember one of my research participants reporting that he was convinced that a man at Manchester Victoria railway station was a spy, because he saw a man '... sending a signal by tapping out a Morse code message with a rolled-up newspaper against his thigh ...'. I can understand why it's tempting merely to see delusional beliefs as symptoms of a psychiatric illness, but a psychological perspective is a little different. We all try to make sense of the world, and we all try to understand why people around us are behaving in odd ways. In these days of terrorist alerts, we welcome vigilance. Mistakenly fearing that there's a plot isn't so outlandish – even if it does cause major problems for the individual.

So part of the story of paranoia involves relatively ordinary errors of judgement. Dan Freeman at Oxford University has commented on how, over many decades and in many different cultures, people have been right to be paranoid.[10] Dan has numerous examples, but one will suffice. Between 1932 and as recently as 1972, researchers in Tuskegee, Alabama, USA, conducted a secret and highly unethical experiment into syphilis. In this horrible experiment, poor African American men thought they were receiving free health care from the US government. Instead, they were identified as having syphilis (which could readily be treated with penicillin), but were not told of the diagnosis and were instead left untreated by the US Public Health Service in order to study the natural progression of untreated syphilis. In other words, you're right to be suspicious, and perhaps especially right to be suspicious if you're black or poor. My research for my PhD investigated a slightly different element of the picture – how people explain negative events. We looked at the pattern of explanations that depressed people made for negative events (and in particular the self-blaming explanations), and contrasted them with explanations made by people with paranoid delusions and people who had no significant mental health issues. We found that paranoid people tended not to make the kinds of self-blaming explanations for negative events that depressed people do. This doesn't, however, mean that avoiding self-blame is always good. We identified at least three different kinds of explanation – internal explanations (blaming yourself – 'it's my fault') but then also two different types of external explanations: external–personal explanations (blaming someone else – 'it's her fault') and external–situational explanations where situational or circumstantial factors are seen as the cause of the problem. Paranoia was particularly associated with external–personal explanations. Not surprisingly, blaming other people for your problems tends to make you paranoid.

HOW FAST DO WE LEARN?

Most of what really matters to us is learned. While our genes give us our brains, and our brains are immensely powerful learning engines, it's the learning that matters. The key problems of poor mental health – paranoia, depression, social anxiety, etc. – are largely the result of poor learning experiences rather than biological deficits.

The human brain has an enormous potential for learning, and it is language that sets humans apart from other animals. Children learn to speak at a prodigious rate. The average adult has a vocabulary of about 10,000 words; apparently, university graduates have an average vocabulary of 17,200, while Shakespeare's might have been as large as 20,000. Although we learn some of those words (the more unusual ones) later in life, most of these words are necessary for everyday life, and we obviously have to learn them quickly. By the age of eighteen months, most children have a vocabulary of about fifty words, and probably understand two or three times as many. Between the ages of eighteen months and about seven years, children learn between five and six new words a day, and between the ages of seven and eleven, about twenty new words each day. To learn an adult vocabulary by the time we grow up, we have to learn at this rate, and most of us manage to do it. However, it is remarkable that we not only learn the meanings of twenty new words a day but also how to use these new words correctly and in context. After children leave school, the number of new words learned each day tends to slow down, but, even then, people's vocabularies grow as they read, talk, discuss things with friends and study. It's a rather sad, if universal, fact that children from wealthier families tend to be exposed to, and possess, larger vocabularies than children from poorer families.

Children learn most of their language naturally and without overt teaching. Very young children imitate the words (and sounds) that they hear. They learn to associate words with actions and objects ('put your coat on') and learn to identify patterns, sequences and repetitions. The American academic Noam Chomsky suggested that children have 'innate grammar'.[11] He meant that at least some of the rules of grammar (or how language works, how words represent things, actions and ideas) are hard-wired into the brain. Chomsky's idea was that children easily learn language because their brains have evolved to understand instinctively the symbolic relationship between words. Although Chomsky is a great academic, with intelligent and powerful political commentary, I think he is mistaken about the idea of innate grammar.

Humans, and perhaps particularly children, have something much more like an innate pattern-detecting, pattern-matching and pattern-making ability. We learn to make sense of the 'blooming, buzzing' confusion of the outside world by seeking out patterns of increasing elegance and complexity. The phrase 'one great blooming, buzzing confusion' comes from William James's great book *The Principles of Psychology*, published in 1890, and describes the way in which a baby is born without any sense of how the world works.[12] We have to learn how to make patterns out of confusion. Some of this can be seen when people gain or regain their sight after long periods of blindness. A typical report is that shapes and figures, recognisable images such as faces, take time to emerge from an unrecognisable kaleidoscope of confusion. We learn to recognise pattern from chaos.

Oddly, it's likely that a great deal of this learning, at least in children, occurs through a reduction of confusion as much as a building of connections. I mentioned the 'pruning' of neural synapses in Chapter 1, because this is how the vast number of connections between the 86 billion neurons present at birth become both added to and also, importantly, trimmed as we age. It has been estimated that a young child has perhaps 150 per cent more synapses than an adult. As we age, as we experience things, as we learn, we prune these synapses and build some new ones. However, it may well be that the pruning of unnecessary connections has an important role in reducing William James' 'blooming, buzzing, confusion' to become a smoother and more logical set of associations.

QUICK LEARNERS

As well as learning language quickly – learning ten or twenty new words every day – we also learn the complex rules of social behaviour very quickly. My son is keen on cycling, and visited a velodrome for the first time a couple of years ago. Cycling (like all sports when you get into them) is a complicated and expensive business. As I'll explain in a later chapter, my son and several members of our family go road cycling regularly, but a velodrome is a different experience because it has a circular wooden track banked at a vertiginous forty-two degree angle. The style of riding is different too, with a different bike (no brakes, a fixed gear) and a greater emphasis on competitive racing. Competitive cycling is a very tactical sport, because tucking in behind another cyclist can save you up to 40 per cent of your energy – the bikes are extraordinary pieces of engineering (that's why they're so expensive) and the main drag on a cyclist is wind resistance. So, tactics on the track are all-important, which means that my son was forced to learn the rules. I stood by the side of the track and watched him set off – there were about fifeen cyclists shooting around the track and practising 'through-and-off'. The cyclist at the front powers ahead but, because she's cutting through the air (and thereby helping those behind), gets tired quickly. So, she peels off to the right, up the velodrome banking, loops around the rest of the following cyclists (the 'peloton') and drops back at the rear of the group. The group continually refreshes itself and builds up speed. My son knew all these basics, but it was obvious to me after a couple of laps that there was a slight problem. The question was, when you've peeled off to the right and gone up the banking, exactly where are you 'supposed' to drop back? The cyclists are powering along at 30 miles per hour and, inevitably, there are gaps and bunches in the group. Is the etiquette for the former leader to drop back at the very end of the peloton, or is he allowed to slot back in where there's a gap? It was obvious to me and my son's grandfather, watching him, that he was a little hesitant on his first run, and his speed suffered a little, but my son then carefully watched what the next couple of people did. When it was his turn at the front (to peel off, go up the banking, drop back in), he very confidently shot off and dropped back into the first available, appropriate space. He clearly didn't want to offend, look inept, clip the wheel of another cyclist (crashes at 30 miles per hour are nasty) or lose speed. All of this complex decision-making with both social reputation and physical safety at stake was factored in through a couple of glances at his fellow cyclists and a few seconds' thought. This is simply a trivial example of how efficient we are at processing these complex social rules.

LEARNED, NOT GIVEN

These complex social rules are certainly not hard-wired products of the brain. There hasn't been remotely enough time for evolution to have produced these as 'instincts'. The range of different social structures around the world and through history also means it's impossible to account for these rules in biological terms.

Clearly, we learn to understand the world in different, divergent ways. Our brains are supremely efficient learning engines. We have evolved the most complicated machines in the known universe, and these hugely powerful organs are particularly well adapted to understanding social rules and relationships. Through all the psychological mechanisms of learning, people learn to understand their world. People observe the interactions and behaviours of others and draw inferences. We are rewarded for our actions (and occasionally punished) for our behaviour, and actively make sense of the world as a result. Perhaps, most importantly, we explicitly teach our children. It's through this route that we are able to pass on the more complex behaviours and skills. This trait of humans, our tendency actively to teach our children, reflects a number of aspects of human psychology. We're embedded in relationships, in social partnership. We're instinctive learning machines. We possess 'theory-of-mind', and we are aware of what our children are thinking. We extract meaning from what we perceive – it matters to us that our children learn about their world.

Our lives can be complex and fast-moving. To help us make rapid decisions and engage positively with the world, we don't tend to analyse each situation with the logical scrutiny of Oxbridge dons. Most human thought seems to be based on simple rules of thumb that permit rapid, if sometimes inaccurate, action. That is, people make many (perhaps most) important decisions using precious little logic but instead relying on heuristics or 'rules of thumb'. This way of thinking allows rapid, practically useful, responses to practical problems, but isn't always strictly logical. Heuristics are simple, efficient rules that help people make decisions and judgements and solve problems, typically when facing complex situations or incomplete information. They can lead to mistakes, and because of this they can contribute to emotional difficulties or other psychological problems, and addressing the consequences of heuristic reasoning is an important element of many psychological therapies such as CBT.

FOUNDATIONS OF THOUGHT

Our frameworks of understanding of the world – our cognitive schemas – tend to be self-sustaining. The way we understand the world is based on the associations and connections that we make, and this tends to mean that we pay attention to, understand and remember information that is consistent with what we already know. We tend to seek out and pay attention to information that makes sense to us, and that means we seek out information that confirms what we were originally thinking.

This tendency can explain some of the details of human behaviour, and especially our prejudices and biases. It makes sense of why the complex but sometimes bizarre belief systems of diverse human cultures tend to maintain themselves. However, it also means that, while we are guided by our framework of understanding of the world, this framework of understanding is also the product of our experiences. Learning and teaching will shape our frameworks for understanding the world, whether that learning is as a result of a strategic, planned attempt to educate us or the circumstantial impact of events. Those frameworks of understanding – the thoughts we have about ourselves, other people, the world and the future – will affect all aspects of our lives.

Humans learn fast, efficiently and elegantly. We rapidly make sense of our environment, impute meaning, and construct abstract representations of the world. These representations may be incorrect, are frequently subject to bias, are usually the product of heuristic, illogical, shorthand rules of thumb. Nevertheless, we are supremely efficient at pattern-matching and sense-making. We don't just react to the world, we understand it.

CHAPTER 3

THE NEW LAWS OF PSYCHOLOGY: PSYCHOLOGY AT THE HEART OF EVERYTHING

Psychology – or how we think about the world – is at the centre of human life. Biological, social and circumstantial factors affect our mental health when they disrupt or alter psychological processes. We may be the product of an interaction between genes and environment, but humans are more than that because we make sense of the world.

It would be wonderful to have a simple, elegant explanation of all mental health problems. Journalists often ask academics deceptively challenging questions about the nature and cause of psychological problems, and we regularly set variants of 'what causes depression?' as an exam question. Both interviewees and students would be delighted to be able to give an answer in a single sentence, but life is more complex than that. Of course, many people offer some variant on 'it's a chemical imbalance' – with all the overt or hidden implications of genetic origins. We very frequently hear people say 'it's an illness', and occasionally 'it's an illness, like any other'. This simple 'disease model' of mental illness is very prevalent and seldom questioned.

The simple answer is attractive: it neatly (if misleadingly) offers a definitive answer and it hints at the wealth of scientific understanding. Such simple explanations imply that there might be a straightforward answer, perhaps a pill to remedy the 'imbalance'. These explanations can be seductively attractive because they appear to attach no blame to the individual or those around them – it's nobody's 'fault' that there's a chemical imbalance. They are particularly attractive because the remedies require little or no effort: the person should obey the doctors, adhere to the regime, and the medicine will do the work; but life is, unfortunately, more complex than that.

A good student, answering our hypothetical examination question, might suggest that the cause of depression (or, for that matter, any other problem) is 'multifactorial', and that biological, psychological and social factors all play a part. It's widely accepted that most complex mental health issues result from some form of a combination of these factors. The UK's National Health Service offers online information about depression that echoes this: it states that 'there is no single cause of depression, and people develop depression for different reasons', before going on to list stressful life events, illness including coronary heart disease, cancer and head injuries, personality traits, social isolation, the use of alcohol and drugs and childbirth (as a risk for the mother, not necessarily the child).[1] They also mention a family history of depression, commenting 'research shows that some genes increase the risk of depression after a stressful life event'. Biological factors, in the form of biochemical or neuroanatomical variables, are important in many mental health problems. They certainly can't be discounted, but are rarely the whole story. Similarly, as we've seen earlier, social factors are important. It's noticeable that what are referred to as psychological factors are often described in slightly vague ways, and I'll expand on this below. This is close to what I'd like to think I'd say if interviewed by a journalist, and it represents the essence of an excellent account of mental health issues used by the European Commission.

THE EUROPEAN COMMISSION GREEN PAPER – 'A MULTIPLICITY OF FACTORS'

In 2005, the European Commission published an important document discussing the kinds of actions and policies that European governments might be expected to undertake to improve mental health care across the continent.[2] As is common in such documents, there was a brief preamble where the authors attempted to define the problems before moving on to discuss solutions. They concluded that: '… for *citizens*, mental health is a resource which enables them to realise their intellectual and emotional potential and to find and fulfil their roles in social, school and working life. For *societies*, good mental health of citizens contributes to prosperity, solidarity and social justice'. The document continues: 'The mental condition of people is determined by a **multiplicity of factors** including biological (e.g. genetics, gender), individual (e.g. personal experiences), family and social (e.g. social support) and economic and environmental (e.g. social status and living conditions.' It's worth noting that the emphasis – the italics and the bold text – is in the original text. This particular document is a policy discussion for bureaucrats, rather than a scientific analysis, so the authors don't develop the idea of 'a multiplicity of factors'.

THE BIOPSYCHOSOCIAL MODEL

A well-read student, answering our hypothetical examination question, might use the term 'biopsychosocial model' and refer to the work of George Engel. In 1977, the journal *Science* published a paper by Engel that introduced this model into discussions of mental health.[3] He recognised that many descriptions or explanations of mental and physical illness reduced the problems to very simplistic biological explanations, and this was particularly true in mental ill health. Depression, anxiety and psychosis were all too frequently seen simply as brain diseases (even if nobody could be too sure what that brain disease actually was). Rather than discussing parenting, love, hopes, fears, relationships, learning and traumatic life events, Engel thought that too many doctors were thinking of mental health purely in terms of neurones, synapses and neuro-transmitters. For Engel, this characterised physical illness too – a heart attack, of course, involves vascular problems in the coronary arteries, but Engel was concerned that social factors in the development of physical health problems (diet, exercise, access to healthcare) and in the consequences of illness (anxiety, depression, losing your job, impact on your family) were being ignored. Engel explicitly hoped his model would provide a scientific account of mental disorder that could challenge these 'reductionist' biological approaches. The biopsychosocial model therefore sees mental disorder as emerging from a human system that has both physical elements (a biological nervous system) and psychosocial elements (relationships, family, community, and the wider society). The concept – and the name – was influential — Engel's original article has been cited at least 4,689 times in scientific papers and yields an impressive 11,300,000 Google hits on the Internet.

The inherent flexibility and capacity of Engel's model to absorb a wide variety of evidence supporting biological, social or psychological influences on mental health meant that different schools of thought pushed and pulled the model in different ways after its publication. Many commentators have welcomed the fact that the biopsychosocial model explicitly acknowledges the role of social factors, because such commentators have routinely railed against biomedical dominance. The challenge, in a world where professionals (and professional bodies) vie for authority and responsibility, of a more social perspective is obvious. Perhaps inevitably, it seems that some more mainstream psychiatrists are concerned that social perspectives lead people away from what they see as the reality of medical, biological, brain-based accounts of mental ill-health. Books or papers with titles such as 'The reality of mental illness', 'A wake-up call for British psychiatry' and (perhaps my favourite) 'Biological psychiatry: is there any other kind?' suggest that at least some people believe that the emphasis on the 'bio' part of the model should take precedence.[4] In practice, discussions of the biopsychosocial model have often, explicitly or implicitly, reserved a dominant position for biomedical approaches – with the social and psychological factors being acknowledged but nevertheless considered to be mere moderators of the direct causal role of biological processes. Indeed, this is a key part of Engel's original paper, in which all the arguments in favour of including psychological and social elements are secondary to a presumed biological basis for disorder. In parallel to this, some psychiatrists have promoted the notion of 'clinical primacy' – the argument that, since mental health problems are primarily medical (it is argued), the medical profession has a primary role. The pressure to promote the medical or biological aspects of such a multifactorial approach has been relentless. Indeed, John Read, an influential clinical psychologist who has recently moved from New Zealand to the UK, has suggested that the bio-psychosocial model should be renamed the 'bio-bio-bio' model, so dominant is this way of thinking.[5]

The biopsychosocial model offers a decent framework for a debate about the cause of mental health problems, but has hardly offered a definitive answer. As a scientific proposition, the biopsychosocial model has a few weaknesses: perhaps most importantly, it doesn't explicitly explain how the relationship between the three types of variable – biological, psychological and social – works in practice. Engel's 1977 paper simply suggests that psychological (or, in his word, 'psychophysiologic') responses to life events interact with 'somatic' or biological factors. This is in part a welcome acknowledgement of the important contribution of psychological and social factors in, as Engel states, many psychological and physical problems. However, the phrasing also clearly reflects an assumption that there is a biological or disease primacy – the responses are 'psychophysiologic' rather than 'psychological' – which ensures that psychological factors are linked to physiological ones. In Engel's words, these responses serve to 'alter susceptibility' to 'diseases' in the context of a genetic predisposition. Phrasing such as this tends to make the reader assume that mental health problems following deprivation, loss or trauma are best thought of in terms of altered susceptibility to a recognised 'disease' that has a genetic basis rather than – as they might otherwise assume – a normal and purely psychological response to the situation. Finally, this statement fails to account for how these entirely different classes of phenomenon interact with each other.

Studies in both animals and humans clearly demonstrate the importance of early, previous and current life experience in the development of problems, and equally (although perhaps significantly Engel didn't feel the need to point this out), research also highlights the role (explained in earlier chapters of this book) of biological factors. We need to think of how these elements — bio-, psycho- and social — relate to one another. The biopsychosocial model is, or should be, more than a simple statement that all three aspects need to be mentioned. A genuinely comprehensive model should be able to explain not only, for example, the role of neurotransmitter abnormalities in depression but also the role of low self-esteem, negative thinking patterns and the findings of greatly increased incidence of mental disorder in disadvantaged groups. Most importantly, how does each class of factor affect the other? In part this is a philosophical question: how can social factors influence biology ... or how can chemicals change your emotions? How – using Engel's phrasing – might psychological factors such as a person's self-esteem or pattern of negative thinking 'interact with existing somatic factors to alter susceptibility and thereby influence the time of onset, the severity, and the course of a disease'? How could a person's income or the number of friends they have affect neurochemistry or the electrical activity of the brain? Equally, to reverse the logic, how could neurochemical influences or genetic susceptibility alter how a person might respond to negative events in their lives? How can one class of philosophical phenomenon – an event, an occurrence – influence another entire class of phenomenon – a biological process? And how can thoughts or beliefs – another class of philosophical phenomenon – affect either? We know that this happens every day. Not only (as Engel reported) does the research literature support this conclusion, but everyday experience bears it out. Our thoughts are always affected by events. Our brains must respond to circumstances, and biology is an important factor in our psychological make-up. It's obvious ... this happens all the time. But how does it work? What is the mechanism?

THE STRESS–VULNERABILITY MODEL

One of the more contentious debates in mental health concerns the nature of 'schizophrenia'. As in almost all mental health problems, most researchers and clinicians believe that the problems that often lead to the diagnosis of 'schizophrenia' result from a combination of brain vulnerabilities (either inherited or acquired) and life events. Genetic vulnerability to psychotic phenomena appears to be multifactorial, caused by interactions of several genes. Equally, there are very many stressful environmental factors – from street drug use through to social adversity and stressful personal relationships – which also appear to be important. Many clinicians and researchers therefore refer to the 'stress–vulnerability' (or stress–diathesis) model developed originally by Joseph Zubin and Bonnie Spring, in 1977.[6]

A website designed by the UK National Health Service to help people experiencing psychotic problems,[7] comments that the stress–vulnerability model '... states that differences in biology and thought processes mean that everybody has individual levels of vulnerability – a threshold. People can be pushed over their threshold and experience psychosis when their resources for coping with stress are exhausted'. The stress–vulnerability model therefore apparently deals with the issue of the interaction between different types of event by describing some as 'vulnerabilities' and some as 'stressors'. There are, however, still problems with this approach. First, reiterating John Read's point about the biopsychosocial model, critics such as Mary Boyle have pointed out that the stress–vulnerability model, commonly interpreted as implying that there is a fundamental biological or genetic vulnerability in schizophrenia, simply takes us back to thinking about biological disease.[8] She even argues that the model may have been developed as a form of defence to guard against potential threats to biological models of 'schizophrenia', and that it is powerful partly because it is deliberately vague. The term 'vulnerability' is somewhat difficult to define and to differentiate from a 'stressor'. For instance, is taking a street drug a vulnerability factor (in that it affects the brain or cognition, making you more vulnerable to subsequent life events) or is it a stressor, and does taking a street drug represent a dangerous stressful event that might interact with a vulnerable brain? While genetic factors might be unequivocal vulnerabilities, any other issues associated with mental health problems are surprisingly difficult to classify as either vulnerabilities or stressors, and are frequently listed as both! It's also somewhat unclear in what way the vulnerabilities and stressors interact. Some researchers appear to assume that they add to each other – that you start off with a certain amount of vulnerability and stress adds to this until it reaches a threshold. Other researchers believe that stress actually alters the vulnerability factors themselves; for instance, social isolation or abusive experiences might actually alter the functioning of the brain, leading to a spiral of the negative consequences of stress.

The stress–vulnerability model is attractive. It is a useful 'heuristic device' (a shorthand or analogy) that gives clinicians and the general public a framework to understand how the huge number of potentially important factors could have combined to cause problems, and indeed what can be done to help. This shouldn't be minimised – the benefits of a simple framework can be enormous because it allows people to talk sensibly about various stressful issues like traumatic life events, the use of drugs and alcohol, and stressful living conditions (e.g. low socioeconomic status, high levels of family conflict) – and it allows people a framework within which to talk about individual differences. Researchers claim that the stress–vulnerability model has stimulated coherent research into mental health problems, and especially social stressors. Clinicians have suggested that the model has helped mental health professionals, family members and clients develop therapeutic interventions and plan care based on addressing potential vulnerabilities and stressors in a systematic fashion.

The stress–vulnerability model is obviously simplistic, and Alison Brabban has used the analogy of a bucket – 'Brabban's Bucket'.[9] The idea is one of water being poured into a bucket, with mental health problems represented as the water overflowing the top of the bucket. A person's vulnerability is reflected in the size or volume of the bucket – the smaller the bucket, the more vulnerable the person (because small buckets fill up more quickly). The stresses are reflected in the water pouring in – more stress equalling more water. The concept of Brabban's Bucket is attractive, but the clarity of Alison's analogy highlights the model's simplicity.

A NEW ACCOUNT – THE MEDIATING PSYCHOLOGICAL PROCESSES MODEL

In 2005, I published a short article in the *Harvard Review of Psychiatry*.[10] For the reasons I've just outlined, I argued that we needed a more rigorous and coherent account of the role of psychological factors in mental health. I argued that, whereas the biopsychosocial model implied that biological, psychological and social factors are coequal partners, disruption of psychological processes is in fact a final common pathway in the development of mental disorder. In what I later termed the 'mediating psychological processes model', I suggested that biological and social factors, together with a person's individual experiences, lead to mental disorder through their combined effects on those psychological processes. This model brings together several of the points I've made earlier in this book.

Nearly everybody suggests that there are multiple, simultaneous factors leading to the development of mental health problems. In such cases, scientists often use the statistical technique of 'multiple regression' to test the degree to which each factor (each 'variable' for statisticians) contributes to the outcome. In the case of mental health, we can imagine a theoretical multiple regression analysis predicting mental health from the biological, psychological and social components of the biopsychosocial model. A simple model of those relationships is shown in Figure 3.1.

With biological factors, social factors and life events predicting mental health, this approach is close to the biopsychosocial model, but rather ignores psychological factors. A possible improvement to this model is illustrated in Figure 3.2.

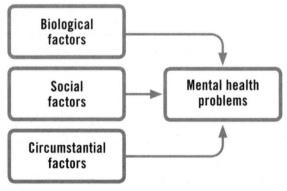

Figure 3.1 A representation of a simplistic biopsychosocial model

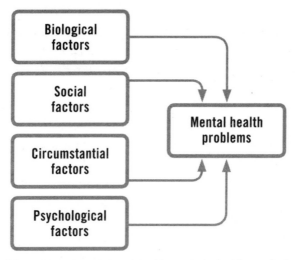

Figure 3.2 A biopsychosocial model with psychological factors included

However, even this improved mode is inadequate, in part because it considers the different variables to be similar in kind or nature, which clearly isn't true. Genetic or biological and environmental factors (whether social or circumstantial) are always in dynamic relationship with each other – it's that dynamic relationship that is at the heart of evolution through natural selection – and the same is true for the relationship between environmental, biological and psychological factors. As we've seen earlier, there is considerable evidence of the existence of a genetic element in many mental health problems, and particularly in those problems that lead to a diagnosis of 'schizophrenia'. Psychotic phenomena, and particularly hallucinations, have been linked with a phenomenon called cerebral lateralisation.

The human brain is clearly divided into two hemispheres, which are slightly different in their physical structures because they aren't exact mirror-images of each other. There is a great deal of discussion about so-called 'right-brain tasks' and 'left-brain tasks', with creativity and art being contrasted with logic and numeracy, for example. Much of this discussion is fanciful, but it is quite clear that many important (if less glamorous) cognitive activities are lateralised – controlled more by one brain hemisphere than the other. The nature of this cerebral lateralisation – the degree to which one hemisphere is more involved in any particular function than another – is complex. Language processes take up a large proportion of the brain's functioning, and many areas of the brain, in both hemispheres, are involved. For instance, grammar and vocabulary appear to be functions lateralised (at least in general terms) to the left hemisphere in most people. On the other hand, functions such as intonation and accent seem to be more functions of the right hemisphere. This complex lateralisation is natural and part of a healthy functioning brain. Several researchers have suggested that people who hear voices are more likely to have poorly lateralised cerebral hemispheres and, in particular, that the brain's language areas are less lateralised. Naturally, it is believed that biochemical, neuroanatomical and, fundamentally, genetic abnormalities lead to poor lateralisation of language processing and hence – presumably – to the problems associated with a diagnosis of schizophrenia.

The story of cerebral lateralisation and hallucinations might give an illustration of the relationship between biological and psychological issues. One key task in neural language processing must be the identification and localisation of perceptual experiences and, clearly, the brain performs this function. We could ask what language functions might be relevant to the experience of hallucinations. There is widespread consensus that auditory hallucinations arise from misattributed cognitions – usually unspoken (or in occasional cases muttered) and unrecognised thoughts – that are not recognised by the individual as being internally generated and, instead, are attributed to external sources. Psychologists refer to the process by which people determine where an experience comes from ('is this my thought, or did I hear it?') as 'source monitoring'. People don't either possess, or lack, this ability; rather, it's a process that operates in different ways for different people in different circumstances. There are many factors (environmental noise, emotional stress, etc.) that can affect source monitoring abilities. If there is a partial failure of lateralisation in the areas of the brain relevant to language processing, this is probably related to the experience of hallucinations as a result of its effect on source monitoring. Indeed, it's very likely that other biological factors act similarly, e.g. street drugs, medication, illness.

This means that biological issues – biological factors that impact on the brain structures related to source monitoring – lead to problems in discriminating voices (heard) from other forms of cognition (thought or remembered) because they disrupt or affect a psychological process – source monitoring. The final, inescapable pathway to hearing disembodied voices is a psychological process – the answer to the question 'did I hear that or imagine it?'. Biological factors are hugely important here because they can affect your ability to make that discrimination. Biological factors can make it difficult for you to tell if a voice is real or not because the mechanism that we use to perform that psychological process is the brain, and the brain is a biological organ. The same is true for the relationship between social or environmental factors and both mental health and hallucinations. Source monitoring is also affected or influenced by factors such as noise, stress, experience of traumatic events, and indeed by those kinds of phenomena that complicate the definitions of biological or environmental, such as street drugs. When stress or noise lead to hallucinations, they do so because they affect the brain's ability to perform the same function. When people experience hallucinations following traumatic events, it seems reasonable that emotional factors and intrusive, automatic, negative thoughts (which are, of course, very common indeed) combine to mean that those thoughts are misinterpreted as voices. Both biological and environmental factors influence mental disorder through their impact on psychological processes.

This type of analysis is not limited to hallucinations. As we saw earlier, abnormalities in serotonin metabolism have been implicated in depression. To give one example of this: the amino acid tryptophan is a dietary precursor of serotonin (the body manufactures serotonin from tryptophan). If you eat a specially designed tryptophan-reducing diet, this can have the knock-on consequence of affecting serotonin levels and induce depression (a rather unpleasant experience). So, clearly, again, biological factors have psychological consequences. Serotonin is implicated, in turn, in the neurological mechanisms supporting various important appraisal processes. Interestingly, while low levels of serotonin may well be extremely bad for us, the role of serotonin in depression is complex. First, when people are happy, their serotonin levels appear to rise ... a reverse of the normal cause and effect relationship of psychiatry. More importantly, serotonin appears to be an important neuro-transmitter related to the processing of information to do with social status, impulsivity, and reward and punishment. All of these issues – your social status, in particular – are key to how people see themselves, their world, and their future – the negative cognitive triad of the cognitive model of depression.

So the biological tryptophan–serotonin system is indeed implicated in depression, but it's a little simplistic to say that 'depression is low serotonin'. If low serotonin levels had no effect on psychological processes, people would not experience the consequences as depression. Equally, if other factors (such as negative life events) were to have a similar effect – to change the way a person thinks about themselves, their world, and their future – low mood would be a natural consequence. In other words, what matters is the effect of all these different factors on psychology: therefore, biological factors appear to have their effect on mental health through psychological processes.

Again, this is true for social or environmental factors. Living in poverty and in conditions of social deprivation can indeed lead to problems such as depression, but living in such a disadvantaged environment may also lead to disillusionment, hopelessness and learned helplessness – to a realisation that there is little or nothing that can be done to improve the situation and that your actions have no effect or purpose. Depression is the direct consequence of this disruption of psychological processes and, finally, the same applies to particular life experiences or circumstances. Being assaulted by your parents would obviously lead to problems, but psychologists would argue that the association between cause (assault) and the effect (mental disorder) is, again, mediated by the disruption of psychological processes. In the case of sexual, emotional or physical abuse, the experience is likely to affect the ways in which the children (and later the adults) see themselves, the people in their lives, their own actions and their consequences, and the ways in which relationships and social intercourse should be governed.

The conclusion of all these arguments is that mental health and well-being are an essentially psychological phenomena, and that biological, social and circumstantial factors operate causally to affect them both by disrupting or disturbing psychological processes. Both nature and nurture are important, and our psychology is the product of nature and nurture, but our psychology is a phenomenon that itself has explanatory power. In 2005, I suggested that this key role for psychology is best expressed in a diagram such as Figure 3.3.

This is a robust, assertive, psychological reformulation of the biopsychosocial model. I started this chapter by discussing variants of the general biopsychosocial model and explained that a multiplicity of biological, social and psychological factors contribute to mental health. I also suggested that merely saying that these factors add together, or are poured into Brabban's Bucket, may be a useful analogy, but it's not a full scientific account. I believe that the most sensible way to account for these relationships is to suggest that biological, social and circumstantial factors have their effect on mental health through their influence on key psychological processes.

This is an assertive model in the sense that it places particular priority on psychological factors. It suggests that mental health and mental well-being are quintessentially a psychological

Figure 3.3 A 'psychobiosocial' model, with psychological factors in their proper relationship to biological, social and circumstantial factors

issue. It means that psychological factors are always implicated in mental health issues. Another way of putting it is that psychological factors are a 'final common pathway' for the development of mental health problems. This is a statement that some might find a little arrogant, but mental health, whatever else it is, involves the behaviour, thoughts and emotions of human beings. Psychology, by definition, is the study of human behaviour, thoughts and emotions. The psychological factors being discussed here are the processes that control those behaviours, thoughts and emotions.

It is important to stress that the 'psychological factors' I refer to in this model include a wide range of quite basic processes, many of which may be relatively unconscious; consequently, the impact of social or biological factors on these psychological processes often happens without any conscious awareness of it (indeed, since the days of Sigmund Freud, we've recognised that many influences on psychology are unconscious). This applies equally to social or biological factors. So, a person whose genetic inheritance has led to less-well lateralised language areas in the brain might have difficulty monitoring the source or origin of mental events. That inheritance could be related to the pattern of making creative and personally salient connections between events that I discussed earlier in the context of Jim van Os's research. Exposure to high levels of stress, street drugs and excessive caffeine intake might also be factors. In these circumstances, as we've seen earlier, the person might be at risk of auditory hallucinations – mistaking internal mental processes for external voices – and is very unlikely to be actively thinking differently in any conscious sense. In fact, part of the problem may be that these processes are generally not amenable to mindful attention. Our information processing system isn't evolved to be conscious – in day-to-day life very few of us are actively thinking 'that's a thought; that's a thought; that's somebody's voice, I didn't think that; that's a thought': the processing is automatic and unconscious. However, the processing – the source monitoring process, the decision as to whether the experience is a voice or a thought – is happening, and it's this processing that is subtly influenced by poor cerebral lateralisation, stress, drugs, etc.

It is extremely difficult to see how these factors could lead to hallucinations without affecting psychological processes. The 'point' of a hallucination is that a person comes to the (automatic, unconscious) conclusion that the experience is 'voice-like' when in fact there is no external voice. If it were suggested that biological factors could lead to hallucinations without affecting some form of psychological process, that would be essentially the same as saying that there is no mental processing involved in coming to that conclusion, which is difficult to imagine. Even more interestingly, if there are no psychological processes involved, that's rather akin to saying that the brain isn't involved (since that's what the brain is for) and it's rather difficult then to imagine how brain-based biology could be involved.

The idea that biological factors affect our mental health through their effect on psychological processes is entirely compatible with the broad thrust of neurological research. In Chapter 1 I discussed the work of Jim van Os and colleagues into the interaction between the environment and genetic factors. They argued that this interaction is associated with psychotic problems through the effect on how children develop 'social world representations' or 'mental representation of the social world'. Forming representations of your social world is a quintessentially psychological issue. Research by Silbersweig and colleagues similarly suggests that depression, panic attacks and hallucinations are clearly associated with particular brain processes, and even that neurological problems associated with those processes can lead to problems. However, these findings clearly also point to the role of psychological processes – the 'evaluation of self-related stimuli ', 'hypervigilance to threat' or 'generating an internal representation of reality'. For these neuroscientists it is important to identify how the neurological abnormalities that have associations with mental health problems might achieve their effects. They do that by making reference to those psychological processes that have, in turn, been associated with mental health problems. So, in the case of anxiety, researchers discuss such things as how the amygdala is associated with hypersensitivity to subtle or unconscious sensory and visceral stimuli – in other words, responding more strongly to subtle signs of threat. All psychological processes – or at least all those psychological processes in the material world open to scientific scrutiny – must involve some grounding in neurology, but the psychological processing of information remains the key part of the puzzle.

Similarly, we might think about a person growing up in socially deprived circumstances, exposed to traumatic or stressful events, and whose genetic heritage may involve subtle anomalies in serotonin metabolism. In these circumstances, people may also tend to feel their actions will have little effect, to imagine themselves to be ineffectual and to find day-to-day experiences rather unrewarding, and so the 'psychological' nature of the processes is perhaps more obvious. It's more commonplace to think of optimism and expectations, whether we blame ourselves for the bad things that happen and how we maintain our self-esteem as 'psychological', although part of the role of a clinical psychologist is to help people become more aware of these links. This helps to understand how depression might have psychological processes as a 'final common pathway'. It's actually very difficult to imagine how either biological or social factors could conceivably lead to mental health problems without invoking psychological processes.

It is certainly true that people frequently experience problems such as lethargy or agitation – these are well-known physical conditions that can affect our mood. One example is anaemia, which is common in women after childbirth and can result in very significant lethargy – a condition that is relatively easily treated by iron tablets. What is interesting about this phenomenon, however, is that there is a qualitative difference between the physical effects of physical problems (such as lethargy), and the psychological consequences (such as depression) that follow when these biological processes start to affect how a person is making sense of their world – how they think about their ability to cope with family life, or worry about their health, for instance. When biological factors make you depressed, that's because the psychological processes that you use to make judgements have been affected and your thoughts about self, world and future have been altered.

WE ARE SHAPED BY OUR THOUGHTS

Our thoughts, emotions and behaviour and, therefore, our mental health, are largely determined by how we make sense of and understand the world, which is not limited to conscious cognitive processes. Over the years, psychologists and psychiatrists have discussed what, in this context, we'd call disruptions or disturbances in other types of psychological processes. The phenomenon of 'learned helplessness' was mentioned earlier when I discussed the impact of both social deprivation and negative life events on our sense of optimism and motivation and it is closely associated with psychological accounts of depression. Recently, cognitive aspects such as a person's explanations of why negative events may have occurred, and optimistic beliefs about the future, have been added to the learned helplessness model. Originally, the learned helplessness model was a purely behavioural phenomenon, based on the behaviour of rats and dogs when faced with inescapable punishment, and had nothing to do with beliefs or thoughts. This doesn't stop it being a psychological account, as there are many highly reputable fields of psychology that do not rely on thoughts, attitudes, beliefs and the rest of the panoply of cognitive psychology (although, for obvious reasons, these discussions are not so likely to reach the pages of popular psychology books for the mass market). Purely behavioural models of depression have a long and distinguished history, and remain highly regarded.

Behavioural interventions are very widely used in mental health care. For people with depression or low mood, activity scheduling is often recommended. This is a very simple concept – a therapist or nurse will work with the client to gather a decent idea of what the person is doing on a day-to-day basis. Very often, and understandably, we find that depressed people are doing very little with their time. It's perhaps a little simplistic, but if you're experiencing a lot of negative events, you need some positive events to generate healthy emotions. It's a vicious circle, and depressed people often don't feel inclined to take part in exercise, to go out, to contact friends, etc. Nurses or therapists often offer 'activity scheduling', which means working with their clients to make a plan for what they might do in their week so that the number of positive activities they engage in is increased. Behavioural models of depression based on the frequency of negative and positive events are usually now further developed by incorporating cognitive elements – the person's thoughts and beliefs – but are still entirely psychological.

Behavioural approaches offer good explanations for many forms of anxiety, and anxiety problems can often be helped effectively through behavioural intervention. Cognitive models are now more common than purely behavioural ones, but behavioural interventions remain very popular. People with various phobias will often be helped by graded exposure, where a person is encouraged (or taught) to use relaxation techniques, and then helped to work through a gently increasing hierarchy of feared situations. This might involve progressing from a picture of a spider in a book, to a plastic spider, then a real but a dead spider, then a live spider in a cage, a small spider on the therapist's hand, a large spider in a cage, a small spider on the client's hand, a large spider on the therapist's hand and, finally, a large spider on the client's hand. Usually, therapists employ a mixture of behavioural approaches and add cognitive elements, such as discussing the client's thoughts and conscious fears, but the point is that the psychological processes don't have to be conscious ones.

Psychodynamic and psychoanalytic approaches also have a distinguished history and have been highly influential on modern psychology and psychiatry. They have their own language, not of thoughts or beliefs, but of 'object relations', 'drives', etc. However, these are still psychological processes, and can be disrupted like any others. Psychotherapists often describe depression, for example, involving anger turned inwards. It is difficult to imagine a so-called 'personality disorder' explained without invoking psychology, but although many psychodynamic accounts simply do not use the language of cognitive psychology, we are still talking about the disruption of psychological processes.

The idea of 'making sense of and understanding the world' is a broad concept, but it does seem clear that the most important issue in mental health is – in Aaron Beck's words – our cognitive triad of thoughts about self, world and future. While all animals make some kind of sense of their world, human beings appear to be unique both in manipulating abstract representations of the world and in being self-aware. So it follows that the most important – and certainly the most interesting – psychological issues are those beliefs and thoughts that are at least partially accessible to consciousness. What we believe about ourselves, our abilities, strengths and weaknesses, what we hope – or fear – for the future, and our beliefs about the nature of the world, especially the social world, are crucial to our mental health.

TESTING THIS IDEA

In the end, scientific ideas are only useful when they can be tested – and when they pass that test. There should be a relatively straightforward set of relationships between biological factors, social and circumstantial factors, psychological factors and mental health and well-being. With the help of the BBC, and along with colleagues Sara Tai, Matthias Schwanneaur and Eleanor Pontin, I was able to test these ideas using an online mental health experiment on the BBC LabUK website.

Over 40,000 people participated in the experiment, which looked at how each of the main factors of the model (biological, circumstantial and social factors, psychological processes and both mental health problems and well-being) related to each other. I am strongly of the opinion that peer-review, scientific journals are the right place to dissect and explore scientific experiments, so I won't go into details of that experiment here. I was, of course, immensely reassured that the (extraordinarily complicated) statistical analysis substantially supported my theory. All of the key factors that were believed to be important in our mental health and well-being were indeed significant.[11] Most importantly, however, the best way of explaining how these factors interrelated was with psychological factors (how we respond to challenges, and how we explain negative life events) mediating the process (see Figure 3.3).

LEARNING INVOLVES PSYCHOLOGICAL MECHANISMS

We are shaped by thought, and our thoughts are shaped by events. The developments in psychology – particularly cognitive psychology – over the past twenty years make it clear that our thoughts, emotions and behaviour (and, therefore, our mental health) are largely determined by how we make sense of and understand the world, which is, in turn, largely determined by our experiences and upbringing. These biological, social and circumstantial factors affect our mental health through their effect on psychological processes.

This relatively simple idea is the essence of clinical psychology as a profession and is – or perhaps should be – the basis of psychotherapy. Clinical psychology has grown rapidly as a profession. It didn't exist before the twentieth century and was still a small profession in 1989, when a report recommended that by the year 2000 there should be as many as 4,000 'healthcare psychologists' employed in the UK's NHS. Now, in 2011, there are nearly 10,000 clinical psychologists in the UK, and about 6,000 psychologists in other branches of the profession (such as forensic psychology, counselling psychology and health psychology). I think it is no accident that this growth in the profession has paralleled the developments in cognitive science described in this book. Clinical psychologists pride themselves on applying the psychological theory they have studied as undergraduates to their work in the clinic. It's perhaps a sign of the success of the scientific developments, understanding better the ways in which people make sense of the world, and how that can sometimes lead to mental health difficulties, that the application has been so successful.

Traditional approaches to psychological therapy can occasionally suffer from using the approach that therapy is (or should be) the same as medication. We often talk as if discussing 'therapy for depression' is conceptually the same as 'antidepressants for depression', but the ideas presented here suggest a rather different approach. Since people's mental well-being is dependent (at least in large part) on their framework of understanding and their thoughts about themselves, other people, the world and the future, helping people think differently about these things can be helpful and should be the basis of therapy. We should not be treating illnesses, but helping people think effectively and appropriately about the important things in life. As I'll discuss later, these ideas aren't dependent on diagnostic distinctions (which I'll mention in a later chapter), and they don't only apply to certain people. There is no such thing as 'abnormal psychology' in the same sense as there is no such thing as 'abnormal physics'. The laws of physics apply universally, but occasionally can explain tragedies. The laws of psychology are similarly universal, and can explain both well-being and distress.

NEW LAWS OF PSYCHOLOGY

Psychology is a scientific discipline. That means (at least for me) that psychologists make hypotheses about how our minds work and then set out to test these ideas. Most scientific disciplines have 'laws': for example, there are the laws of thermodynamics (which many creationists seem to misunderstand) and Newton's Laws, such as 'every action has an equal and opposite reaction' (a phenomenon that leads to amusing YouTube videos of people firing shotguns without thinking about the recoil), and the laws of gravitational attraction. Psychology has very few 'laws': probably the only 'law' that most psychologists can remember is the Law of Effect. As I mentioned earlier, this is very important – it states that, if an action is followed by a reinforcing, positive consequence, it is *more* likely that it will be repeated, whereas, if an action is followed by a punishing, negative consequence, it is *less* likely that it will be repeated. It has helped shape a wide range of policies and practices, from childcare and education to criminal justice policies. But I believe it's now possible to summarise all these ideas in two new laws of psychology:

Law 1. Our thoughts, emotions and behaviour (and, therefore, our mental health and well-being) are largely determined by how we make sense of the world.

Law 2. How we make sense of the world is largely determined by our experiences and up-bringing.

CHAPTER 4

THINKING DIFFERENTLY:
DIAGNOSIS

A few years ago, Erika Setzu and I, together with colleagues at the University of Liverpool, conducted a simple research study into serious mental health problems. We asked people who either had been, or were currently, in great distress and had been admitted to acute psychiatric units, about their own understanding of the circumstances of being admitted to hospital. One interview went as follows:

ERIKA: 'Do you know why the problems began?'
INTERVIEWEE: 'No, I don't know for certain. I had taken some pot before my first admission and I thought somebody might have dropped some acid on it. I also had a difficult childhood. I was physically and emotionally abused, sexually abused as well. This is very difficult for me to get my head round.'

A little later, the interview continued:

INTERVIEWEE: 'I started to hear voices, but they were not nice voices, they were horrible.'
ERIKA: 'Did you recognise them?'

INTERVIEWEE: 'It was the man that abused me ... I met this man that was a builder, in construction, you know? And he said that he wanted to give me a job, but they were all lies, he was trying to con me. He took me back to his house, he locked the door and he had sex with me ... And then other voices as well. I went to ... hospital and the nurses were very good to me.'

ERIKA: 'When you went to hospital what did they say was wrong with you?'

INTERVIEWEE: 'Schizophrenia, paranoid schizophrenia.'

ERIKA: 'What do you think personally?'

INTERVIEWEE: 'What do you mean?'

ERIKA: 'Do you think it is what you've got?'

INTERVIEWEE: 'Oh yes, that's what I have got.'[1]

I don't think anybody did anything wrong here (apart from the people who physically, emotionally and sexually abused him). I think that it is right and proper that the interviewee approached medical staff for help, and I have no doubt that they cared for him well. I actually think that both hospital care and even medication may well have been helpful. We know, it's foolish to deny, that people can sometimes become so distressed by the consequences of abuse – such as post-traumatic 'flash-back' memories – and by auditory hallucinations that it's unfair merely to leave them to their own devices. Although admission to psychiatric hospitals can be stressful and distressing, it is occasionally necessary, and I don't take issue with the use of psychiatric medication – when appropriately used. If people are very distressed, medication can be a relief, especially if it targets those neurological mechanisms that underpin the source-monitoring problems that may contribute to the experience of hallucinations. However, to describe this man's experiences as 'paranoid schizophrenia' profoundly misses the point. The technical accuracy of the diagnosis, within the standard diagnostic systems, of 'paranoid schizophrenia' is probably the most appropriate one. But what he describes is humanly understandable and so he doesn't need to be labelled in this way. His childhood history was one of physical, emotional and sexual abuse, some street-drug use, and traumatic, sexual, assaults in adulthood. He describes how the last rapist's voice re-appeared as hallucinations, accompanied by other voices that he – in this context – appears to link to his traumatised childhood. Moreover, this account seems to have a great deal of explanatory power, and so it seems strange to imply that, in some way, the 'illness' of 'paranoid schizophrenia' has caused these voices (especially as nobody knows what is supposed to cause paranoid schizophrenia).

The ancient Greek philosopher Plato once suggested that natural science was the art of 'carving nature at its joints', by which he meant that we need to identify and classify the phenomena – the birds, animals, plants and insects, the minerals, elements and forces – that shape the natural world.

In many branches of science – in geology, botany and biology, in particular – this means an emphasis on classification. For psychiatry, in its infancy in the nineteenth century, medical classification based on scientific principles offered real potential benefits. Early psychiatrists were faced with the same challenges as modern psychiatrists – large numbers of very distressed patients with complicated, changing problems in a pattern of great social deprivation. One of the most influential early psychiatrists was Emil Kraepelin, who in 1919 attempted to reclassify the confusing array of mental conditions into two broad illnesses: 'dementia praecox' (Latin for loss of intelligence before the onset of old age, a term later replaced by 'schizophrenia') and 'manic-depression'.[2]

Today, of course, we have a significant legacy of psychiatric diagnosis, but we still need to address a basic challenge. One that follows directly from Plato is if natural science depends on 'carving nature at its joints', where are those 'joints'? In fact, are there any 'joints'? Is it actually possible to make those kinds of categorical decisions in the field of mental health at all?

I think that these debates were rather elegantly summarised in a remarkable editorial in *The Times* of Saturday 22 July 1854:

> Nothing can be more slightly defined than the line of demarcation between sanity and insanity. Physicians and lawyers have vexed themselves with attempts at definitions in a case where definition is impossible. There has never yet been given to the world anything in the shape of a formula upon this subject which may not be torn to shreds in five minutes by any ordinary logician. Make the definition too narrow, it becomes meaningless; make it too wide, the whole human race are involved in the drag-net. In strictness, we are all mad as often as we give way to passion, to prejudice, to vice, to vanity; but if all the passionate, prejudiced, vicious, and vain people in this world are to be locked up as lunatics, who is to keep the keys to the asylum?[3]

I think there are three key points here. First, a point I shall return to in this chapter – that categorical diagnosis in the field of mental health is unreliable and invalid. As this editorial suggests, we are unable to agree, reliably and validly, on the presence or absence of madness – the 'line of demarcation between sanity and insanity'. This leads directly to the second point, which is that there appears to be a continuum on these issues. Some people, of course, have huge problems, but we're discussing the wide range of human distress encompassed by depression, anxiety, psychosis, etc. There are clear continua in all these experiences: some people are mildly anxious, and other people are so crippled by obsessions and compulsive rituals that their lives are very difficult indeed. Most of us will have had unusual perceptual experiences from time to time, but some people are plagued by continual psychosis. We all get down from time to time, but low mood is so extreme for some people that they contemplate suicide. Madness and sanity are not so much different states as different ends of common spectrums. Madness lies at one end of a continuum – that delightful and utopian state in which we are entirely free from passion, prejudice, vice and vanity lie at the other. However, the author of this editorial also expressed another fascinating and fundamental point, which is that the issues that lead to madness are aspects of normal psychology. So the journalist is suggesting – rightly in my opinion – that madness or insanity emanate from passion, prejudice, vice and vanity. In other words, normal psychological phenomena can affect our thinking to the extent that we blur the line of demarcation between sanity and insanity. After more than twenty years of experience studying and researching mental health, helping clients with a wide range of problems and working at the cutting edge of mental health in the twenty-first century, I think this is right. Although it might be a slightly alarming thought that what we sometimes refer to as madness is just an aspect of normal psychology.

On the face of it, there are good reasons to attempt to classify and describe psychological problems. If the classification were valid and reliable, classification of mental disorders might allow the causes and origins, as well as the nature, of the disorders to be understood. If you could reliably and validly identify a group of people with a particular disorder, investigation of their medical status or life histories might reveal a particular brain abnormality, a particular biochemical imbalance, a particular set of life experiences or a particular pattern of thought that could then explain the origins of that particular disorder. Since this general approach has been successful in other branches of medicine, it makes sense to assume it could apply in psychiatry.

Reliable and valid classification would be useful for researchers too. It would allow them clearly to describe what it is that they are studying. Replicability is vital in science: anyone reading scientists' accounts of their work should be able to understand what they have done and reproduce their experiment. Decent diagnostic classification systems would allow researchers in mental health to define their subject matter appropriately and provide a common language: with such a shared language, researchers could communicate their findings meaningfully.

For medical psychiatrists, in particular, it is important clearly to define the illnesses and conditions that they are trying to treat. If it is possible to make valid and reliable diagnoses, then the appropriate treatment should follow. Assuming that the diagnoses are valid, treatments should be effective. Moreover, it's clear that many people actively want their doctor to offer a diagnosis. It's a slightly odd phenomenon that people seem to be reassured by medical diagnoses that appear to be nothing more than a very brief repetition – in Latin – of the problem that they took to the doctor. A person may go to a doctor complaining that their hair is falling out and are told that they have 'alopecia NOS', which is shorthand for 'not otherwise specified'. They may even be told that it is 'stress-related', without a full discussion of what 'stress' might mean in this context. The person has gone to their doctor reporting that their hair is falling out, the doctor has translated that into 'alopecia' and the patient feel somehow reassured by this. It's perhaps significant that the diagnoses are often in Latin or Greek, which are the languages of tradition, of sapiential authority, of antiquity and of the clerics, and they carry a lot of symbolic weight.

Of course, this is more than just a diagnosis for the individual concerned. The tone of voice and the non-verbal behaviours are signalling that the doctor has heard and, to a degree, understood the problems. The technical, slightly obscure language indicates that the doctor is an expert in the field, and conveys confidence. All of this may be misplaced, of course, but it should be remembered that naming something is an important psychological event. Giving a name to your distress serves a function. However, despite these potential or possible benefits, a cool and dispassionate look at the data suggests it may be difficult to make valid and reliable diagnoses of psychological problems.

HOW ARE PSYCHOLOGICAL DISORDERS CLASSIFIED?

Diagnostic Classification – The Disease Model

The classification of mental health problems and psychological problems is so strongly linked to the medical diagnosis of physical illness, and the medical sub-specialty of psychiatry is so dominant, that the diagnosis and classification of mental illnesses traditionally happens in a similar way to the way that physical illnesses are diagnosed. Problems are seen as symptoms of an illness, and a particular combination of 'symptoms' is seen as evidence of a particular underlying mental illness, which is assumed to be the cause of the identified symptoms. There are two major international classificatory systems for the classification and diagnosis of mental health problems.

THE WORLD HEALTH ORGANIZATION'S INTERNATIONAL STANDARD CLASSIFICATION OF DISEASES, INJURIES AND CAUSES OF DEATH, AND THE AMERICAN PSYCHIATRIC ASSOCIATION'S DIAGNOSTIC AND STATISTICAL MANUAL

One of the first actions of the newly created World Health Organization was, in 1948, to publish a comprehensive list of the world's diseases and illnesses. The International Standard Classification of Diseases, Injuries and Causes of Death (ICD), naturally included psychological and psychiatric conditions (effectively ensuring that these kinds of problems were seen as the responsibility of medicine) and, again naturally, were classified and categorised. For reasons that I'll explain below, this document has been extensively revised over the years, and we are now using ICD-10, the tenth and most recent revision.[4] The latter is, technically at least, the international standard classification system, recommended for administrative and epidemiological purposes, and forms the basis of UK National Health Service statistical procedures.

The immediate post-war period also saw the publication of the American Psychiatric Association's *Diagnostic and Statistical Manual* – DSM,[5] which described the classification system based on the administrative scheme used by the US Army in World War II. Since then, ICD and DSM have run in parallel and there remains considerable overlap between the two systems. As with ICD, the DSM system has been revised and re-edited over time, meaning that the current edition is the fifth – DSM-5. The DSM franchise is, of course, very widely used in the USA, because it is recommended for research classification as well as epidemiological and statistical purposes, and because most researchers want to publish their results in US-based, English-language publications. It has also become standard practice for researchers, even in Europe, to use DSM-IV criteria. With the huge controversy over these diagnostic approaches,[6] it remains to be seen whether DSM-5 will prove to be as dominant.

Two Definitions of Depression

A good illustration of both the overlap and the differences between ICD-10 and DSM-5 can be seen in their diagnostic criteria for depression. ICD-10 guidelines first offer a list of 'typical symptoms', such as depressed mood, loss of interest and enjoyment, and reduced energy, and a list of 'other common symptoms', including reduced concentration and attention, reduced self-esteem and self-confidence, ideas of guilt and unworthiness, bleak and pessimistic views of the future, ideas or acts of self-harm or suicide, disturbed sleep and diminished appetite. ICD-10 gives additional criteria for the diagnosis of 'mild', 'moderate' and 'severe depressive episode'. For a 'severe depressive episode', all three of the 'typical' symptoms should be present, plus at least four other symptoms, some of which should be of severe intensity. The depressive episode should usually last at least two weeks, but if the symptoms are particularly severe and of very rapid onset, it may be justified to make this diagnosis after less than two weeks. If a person presented to a competent healthcare professional (you don't have to be a doctor to make a diagnosis), and reported these problems, then a diagnosis of 'severe depressive episode' would be considered appropriate. The ICD-10 criteria for a 'depressive episode' are listed below.

The DSM-5 diagnostic guidelines are more complex, more detailed and more prescriptive. To make a diagnosis of DSM-5

ICD-10 Depressive Episode

The criteria for diagnosis differ for mild, moderate and severe depressive episode.

For severe depressive episode, all three of the 'typical' symptoms (see below) should be present, plus at least four other symptoms, some of which should be of severe intensity. For mild depressive episodes, at least two of the 'typical' symptoms should be present, but none to an 'intense degree'. For moderate depressive episodes, two of these key symptoms must be present, and to a 'marked degree'. The depressive episode should usually last at least two weeks, but if the symptoms are particularly severe and of very rapid onset, it may be justified to make this diagnosis after less than two weeks.

Typical Symptoms

In typical depressive episodes the individual usually suffers from

1   depressed mood,
2   loss of interest and enjoyment,
3   reduced energy.

Other Common Symptoms are:

(a) reduced concentration and attention;
(b) reduced self-esteem and self-confidence;
(c) ideas of guilt and unworthiness (even in a mild type of episode);

(d) bleak and pessimistic views of the future;
(e) ideas or acts of self-harm or suicide;
(f) disturbed sleep;
(g) diminished appetite.

'major depressive episode', nine key symptoms are listed: (i) depressed mood most of the day, nearly every day; (ii) markedly diminished interest or pleasure in all, or almost all, activities most of the day, nearly every day; (iii) significant weight loss when not dieting or weight gain (e.g. a change of more than 5 per cent of body weight in a month), or decrease or increase in appetite nearly every day; (iv) insomnia or hypersomnia nearly every day; (v) psychomotor agitation (fidgety activity such as pacing up and down) or retardation (the opposite: feeling slowed up and sluggish) nearly every day; (vi) fatigue or loss of energy nearly every day; (vii) feelings of worthlessness or excessive or inappropriate guilt nearly every day; (viii) diminished ability to think or concentrate, or indecisiveness, nearly every day; and (ix) recurrent thoughts of death (not just fear of dying), recurrent suicidal thoughts or a suicide attempt or a specific plan for committing suicide. To receive a diagnosis of 'major depressive episode', five (or more) of these symptoms must have been present during the same two-week period, and must represent a change from previous functioning. At least one of the symptoms present must have been either depressed mood or loss of interest or pleasure. In addition, in DSM-5, there are several additional criteria: the symptoms shouldn't meet the criteria for other disorders (which would offer a more appropriate diagnosis), shouldn't be due to some substance such as drugs or medication, nor be the physical effects of a medical condition. Very importantly, the identified problems must cause clinically significant distress or impairment in social, occupational or other important areas of functioning.

A close inspection of the two definitions is revealing. They are clearly pointing in the same general direction, but it would clearly be possible for a person to meet the ICD-10 criteria for a diagnosis of depression, but fail to meet the DSM-5 diagnosis: the DSM-5 diagnosis is a little more restrictive. For example, a man could present to his family doctor and, entirely honestly, say that he had been experiencing low mood, a loss of interest and enjoyment, and reduced energy for the past three weeks. He would, therefore, be eligible for an ICD-10 diagnosis of 'depressive episode'. However, if he told his doctor that he hadn't experienced any weight loss, was sleeping well, had not experienced any sense of agitation, didn't feel particularly worthless or guilty, was more or less able to concentrate as normal and didn't have any suicidal thoughts, he would not qualify for a DSM-5 diagnosis of 'major depressive episode'.

The fact that ICD and DSM diagnoses differ is a source of embarrassment to psychiatric authorities. In fact, one of the principal reasons for the revision of DSM-IV to become DSM-5 was to permit easier 'read-across' between the two systems. It is embarrassing because if there is an objective illness of 'depression' it would seem odd if social factors – whether you follow an American or European tradition – were to determine its existence. I remain confused by the fact that there are two different diagnostic systems and a mechanism for translating DSM codes into ICD codes. It seems to me that it is unnecessary to have two systems if it is possible to translate between the two systems in this manner. Is it possible that commercial and professional pressures lead mental health professionals to both create and update diagnostic systems?

There have been many specific changes as the DSM franchise has been updated from DSM-IV to DSM-5. One particularly contentious change – and the subject of a critical editorial in the *Lancet* – was the decision to drop a specific exclusion criterion. In the fourth edition, it was technically impossible to diagnose a 'major depressive episode' unless 'the symptoms are not better accounted for by Bereavement' – this requirement was dropped in DSM-5.

Many commentators thought that this was worrying because manuals such as DSM-5 are designed to diagnose mental illnesses. It is a matter for concern that a person grieving for a loved one could be diagnosed with a major depressive episode. The issue is complex because, first, the ICD-10 doesn't have such an exclusion, so in some ways this brings the two manuals closer together. However, since the DSM-IV diagnosis included bereavement as an exclusion criterion, if a person were suffering from low mood and sleeping difficulties, but had suffered the death of a loved one recently, officially the diagnosis of 'major depressive episode' would not be appropriate. This is important because pharmaceutical companies are showing an interest in 'treating' bereavement. A drug called Wellbutrin, which has been prescribed without too much success for a range of problems – from helping people to stop smoking cigarettes to a treatment for premenstrual syndrome – has recently been tested as a specific treatment for low mood in circumstances of bereavement. The easy slide from diagnoses to medical treatment is disturbing.[7]

This general pattern is repeated across many different diagnoses in the two classificatory systems. The diagnostic criteria for schizophrenia, for example, also differ between DSM-5 and ICD-10. These differences might be relatively minor – the mention of 'thought echo, thought insertion or withdrawal, and thought broadcasting' in the case of ICD-10 without a parallel in DSM-5, and a difference between the use of phrases such as 'persistent hallucinations' and 'hallucinations'. However, these differences matter because they determine whether or not treatment is offered, and whether the patient is labelled as 'mentally ill' or being apparently 'sane'. The ICD-10 criteria for a diagnosis of 'schizophrenia' are listed below.

ICD-10 Schizophrenia

A diagnosis of schizophrenia is reached if the individual has a minimum of one very clear symptom (and usually two or more if less clear-cut) from (a) to (d) below, or symptoms from at least two of groups (e) to (h). These should have been clearly present for most of the time during a period of one month or more.

(a) thought echo, thought insertion or withdrawal, and thought broadcasting;

(b) delusions of control, influence, or passivity, clearly referred to body or limb movements or specific thoughts, actions, or sensations; delusional perception;

(c) hallucinatory voices giving a running commentary on the patient's behaviour, or discussing the patient among themselves, or other types of hallucinatory voices coming from some part of the body;

(d) persistent delusions of other kinds that are culturally inappropriate and completely impossible, such as religious or political identity, or superhuman powers and abilities (e.g. being able to control the weather, or being in communication with aliens from another world);

(e) persistent hallucinations in any modality, when accompanied either by fleeting or half-formed delusions without clear affective content, or by persistent over-valued ideas, or when occurring every day for weeks or months on end;

(f) breaks or interpolations in the train of thought, resulting in incoherence or irrelevant speech, or neologisms;

(g) catatonic behaviour, such as excitement, posturing, or waxy flexibility, negativism, mutism, and stupor;

(h) 'negative' symptoms such as marked apathy, paucity of speech, and blunting or incongruity of emotional responses, usually resulting in social withdrawal and lowering of social performance; it must be clear that these are not due to depression or to neuroleptic medication;

(i) a significant and consistent change in the overall quality of some aspects of personal behaviour, manifest as loss of interest, aimlessness, idleness, a self-absorbed attitude, and social withdrawal.

RELIABILITY AND VALIDITY OF DIAGNOSES – RELIABILITY

In scientific terms, the classification and diagnosis of mental illnesses could be appropriate if it is both reliable and valid. Reliable, in this context, means that two people will agree on which diagnosis to use, or would come to the same decision if the process of diagnosis were repeated. There are several things that could lead people to make unreliable diagnoses: the *psychiatrists* (or whoever is making the diagnosis) might behave differently; the *clinical examination* might be different each time; and the people whose problems are being assessed might differ (they might mention different things, behave differently or their problems might even have changed over time). Importantly for formal diagnostic systems, error or unreliability might enter if there were different rules for combining symptoms or different systems of naming and styles of reporting, for example, in different countries.

Researchers looking at these issues in the 1950s and 1960s tended to find that, even when looking at very broad categories of disorder (such as distinguishing depression from anxiety), clinicians tended to agree on diagnoses less frequently than would be desirable.[8] Moreover, as we have seen when looking at the specific criteria for depression, diagnoses can be very specific and, in fact, differentiate between different types of depression, and different types of anxiety. When the reliability of these more precise classifications was examined, it appeared (again several years ago) to be very low. Of more concern is that the reliability coefficients for diagnoses under the DSM franchise appear to be falling steadily over time – it is getting progressively worse with each new edition.[9] It does appear that some diagnoses are more reliable than others, and psychiatric diagnoses are not necessarily any more unreliable than some physical or medical diagnoses. Doctors may be correct in the cause of death on only two-thirds of occasions when their judgements are compared with the results of post-mortems, and even diagnoses of, for example, tonsillitis can be less reliable than those for schizophrenia. The difference, of course, is that there are pathological tests – post-mortem examinations, histology, biological laboratory tests – for most biomedical diagnoses, whereas there are no laboratory tests for mental health problems.[10]

It was precisely because of these early difficulties with unreliable diagnosis that so much detailed effort was channelled into improving the consistency of diagnosis. This is the main reason why both the ICD and DSM have repeatedly been updated, and each revision has been made for a number of reasons, but a major impetus was the need to make diagnoses reliable. Scientific analysis of the sources and causes of unreliability was partly responsible for guiding these revisions. A major research project examining psychiatric diagnosis in the USA and the UK found that Americans were far more likely to be diagnosed with schizophrenia than British citizens, although the opposite was true for manic depression. Considerable steps were taken to ensure that the ways in which the individual symptoms were defined were tightened and the rules for grouping these together into diagnoses were clarified and, to a degree, these efforts were successful. When specific criteria for the two disorders were drawn up, and the clinicians were trained in how to use them, the reliability improved significantly. America and the UK now seem to have very similar rates for the use of the diagnosis of schizophrenia following these revisions, which were fed into the new editions of both DSM and ICD.

Agreement between psychiatrists and, in fact, anyone making diagnoses can also be improved if they not only use specific classification rules but also use standardised interview guides. In the field of mental health, the criteria consist of descriptions of behaviours, thoughts and emotions. In nearly all cases, these can't be independently verified and are subjective judgements – the degree to which a person's 'low mood' constitutes a problem that can 'cause clinically significant distress or impairment in social, occupational, or other important areas of functioning' is partly a matter of judgement. It follows that a standardised interview schedule can significantly improve reliability – the person is asked standardised questions about the diagnostic symptoms and the answers are subjected to the carefully drafted criteria for deriving diagnostic symptoms. This means that the diagnoses are more likely to be reliable because different interviewers will still tend to come to the same diagnosis from the same interview responses.

Diagnoses tend to be statistically reliable in research projects, where standardised interviews tend to be used and where the diagnostic criteria tend to be followed strictly. However, these efforts have had only limited success in normal clinical practice, where diagnosis remains very unreliable. This is partly because clinicians appear to use such standardised interview approaches only very infrequently, and tend to use more idiosyncratic approaches to the rules for deciding upon diagnosis.

RELIABILITY AND VALIDITY OF DIAGNOSES – VALIDITY

As well as being reliable, diagnostic classifications should also be valid – scientifically meaningful and representing real 'things'. Clearly, reliability and validity are closely related: if a diagnosis cannot be agreed upon, or if the same person is given different diagnoses at different times or by different doctors, all the different possible alternatives cannot all be 'real'.

In order to examine these principles more clearly, let us consider an imaginary 'illness' – Kinderman's Syndrome, which is diagnosed by the following 'symptoms': thinning brown hair, a south-east English accent and protruding ears. This diagnosis could be quite reliable because a particular person (let's call him Peter) is likely to be assessed as meeting the diagnostic criteria for Kinderman's Syndrome each time he is interviewed (he is unlikely to change his hair colour and the size of his ears). Two different raters are likely to agree on the presence or absence of the 'symptoms' and, if there is any doubt, very strict criteria could be agreed, specifying exactly what a 'south-east English accent' or 'protruding ears' meant. We could even define the exact shade of 'brown' we meant (which could be very useful as the candidate gets older and greyer). The reliability of the 'syndrome' could be of a satisfactory level – we could easily compare people against the criteria and we'd agree on whether the criteria are met.

However, is this valid? Is there in any real sense a syndrome identified by these criteria? The idea that there might be a syndrome – 'Kinderman's syndrome' – can't be justified merely because we can first list a set of criteria and then reliably agree on whether they are present or not. Obviously, there is no real or valid illness called Kinderman's Syndrome, and the fact that we can invent it and then even diagnose it reliably does not make it valid.

It is entirely possible to invent invalid diagnoses. We have done it before. Although it's fair to say that the diagnosis never really took hold in psychiatrists' imaginations. The nineteenth-century American doctor Samuel Cartwright seriously proposed the diagnosis of 'drapetomania',[11] which was a quasi-medical explanation for the supposedly inexplicable tendency of slaves to attempt to escape from their captors. According to Cartwright, their desire for freedom was a symptom of a mental illness, drapetomania (the Greek word *drapetes* means a runaway slave). In a paper entitled 'Diseases and peculiarities of the negro race', Cartwright suggested that drapetomania was the result of people either treating their slaves as equals or, alternatively, with cruelty. He argued that the Bible said that slaves must be submissive to their masters and so it was madness to wish to run away. Cartwright further argued for preventative measures – if slaves were showing signs of being unhappy, Cartwright prescribed 'whipping the devil out of them' as a 'preventative measure'. Clearly this is an invalid diagnosis – there is no such 'illness' as drapetomania. So how valid are other psychiatric diagnoses: have we made up other invalid concepts? Some easy targets present themselves immediately.

ILL, OR ADOLESCENT?

DSM-5 includes – somewhat incredibly – a diagnostic category of 'oppositional defiant disorder', which is supposedly appropriate for children. The criteria for oppositional defiant disorder are summarised as 'a pattern of negativistic, hostile, and defiant behaviour lasting at least 6 months'. More detailed criteria include: actively defying or refusing to comply with adults' requests or rules, deliberately annoying people, blaming other people for his or her mistakes or misbehaviour, and being angry and resentful. These are, in DSM-5, grouped into three types: angry/irritable mood, argumentative/defiant behaviour, and vindictiveness.

As a parent, I recognise that children can be difficult, and perhaps unhappy, and sometimes they can be vindictive. I'm genuinely not making light of those occasions when children and their parents are desperately, painfully unhappy, and I'm absolutely convinced that these situations can have terrible consequences for children and their parents. However, the 'diagnostic criteria' for ODD do appear to imply that many ordinary children (in fact, both of my own) would be labelled as having a 'disorder'. They imply not only that these issues are problems but also that they are 'symptoms of mental illness'. I don't like it when children are defiant, refuse to comply with my requests or act in a vindictive manner, but does the fact that my daughter is naughty mean she is mentally ill?

These validity arguments also apply to the contentious issue of 'personality disorder'. Personality disorders, in general, are defined as 'long-standing patterns of maladaptive behaviour that constitute immature and inappropriate ways of coping with stress or solving problems'. Examples of personality disorder include: antisocial personality disorder, paranoid personality disorder, narcissistic personality disorder, schizoid personality disorder, etc. Antisocial personality disorder is particularly interesting in the context of the validity of diagnoses of mental disorder, not only because they illustrate the weird circularity of these ideas but also because the UK government has linked an entire programme – the Dangerous and Severe Personality Disorder Programme, designed to help manage very seriously dangerous offenders – on this concept. Do people behave badly because they are suffering from 'Antisocial Personality Disorder' or are they given the label 'Antisocial Personality Disorder' because they behave badly?

DO LABELS EXPLAIN ... OR MERELY LABEL?

In many ways, 'Antisocial personality disorder' illustrates the basic and essential nature of diagnosis. It is often assumed that diagnoses reflect real causal entities, that there really is a 'thing' called 'depression' that causes you (if you develop it) to become withdrawn, lethargic and sad. This is very importantly different from the logical alternative – that people occasionally become withdrawn, lethargic and sad for all kinds of reasons and that to attach the label of 'depression' to that has no explanatory power whatsoever.

'Antisocial personality disorder' refers to a pattern of antisocial acts such as assaults, lying, deceit, etc. Clearly, unambiguously, these things – the individual incidents – are 'real', and the consequences are significant. It may well be the case that people who behave in this way are those who tend to behave in these ways throughout their lives (although this is a slightly more contentious point). The idea that it is possible to invent a 'disorder' such as 'antisocial personality disorder' should not be taken as evidence that there is a real 'thing' out there causing the person to be antisocial.

The label is nothing more than that – a short-hand description. People do not do bad things *because* they have 'Antisocial personality disorder'; the 'disorder' isn't causing the behaviour. The 'disorder' is merely a label for behaviour that has other (perfectly understandable) causes. People are labelled in this way because it appears to serve some function to do so, but it may well be misleading and invalid. The DSM-5 diagnostic criteria for 'Antisocial personality disorder' are listed below.

Diagnostic Criteria (DSM-5) for Antisocial Personality Disorder

Antisocial personality disorder is characterised by a lack of regard for the moral or legal standards in the local culture. There is a marked inability to get along with others or abide by societal rules. Individuals with this disorder are sometimes called psychopaths or sociopaths.

A. Significant impairments in personality functioning:

1. Either;
    a. Egocentrism; self-esteem derived from personal gain, power or pleasure, or;
    b. Goals based on personal gratification; law-breaking and a failure to follow normal rules for social behaviour.
    AND
2. Either;
    a. Lack of concern for the feelings, needs or suffering of others; lack of remorse, or;
    b. Inability to form mutually intimate relationships, use of exploitation, deceit, coercion, dominance or intimidation to control others.

B. 'Pathological' personality traits in the following domains:

1. Antagonism, characterised by:
    a. Manipulativeness,
    b. Deceitfulness,
    c. Callousness,
    d. Hostility,

2. Disinhibition, characterised by:
    a. Irresponsibility,
    b. Impulsivity,
    c. Risk taking.

C. These problems are relatively stable across time and consistent across situations.
D. These problems are not considered normal for the person's age and social background.
E. These problems are not a consequence of substance use or a medical condition.
F. The person is at least 18 years old.

ON BEING SANE IN INSANE PLACES

Making a psychiatric diagnosis suggests that the behaviours and problems – the 'symptoms' – are different from normal life. Many people would consider that a 'diagnosis' of problems that are essentially normal behaviour, is a blow to the validity of the concept.

One much-reported experiment that – at least for some – speaks to the invalidity of the diagnostic approach was conducted in 1973 by David Rosenhan.[12] In a study published under the title 'On being sane in insane places', Rosenhan arranged for eight ordinary people from conventional backgrounds to present themselves to a number of psychiatrists at hospitals in the USA. In each case the individuals complained of hearing disembodied voices saying 'empty', 'hollow' or 'thud'. Apart from complaining of this distressing 'symptom' (which is, of course, a conventional criterion for the diagnosis of schizophrenia), the eight confederates were told to reply to all questions honestly.

All eight individuals were admitted to hospital, and the majority received the diagnosis of schizophrenia. Once they were admitted the 'pseudopatients' behaved normally: they spent their time reading, writing and exploring their new environment. It seemed, however, that the setting and the fact that they had received a diagnosis of mental disorder appeared to affect the way in which these behaviours were reported and interpreted. Staff noted that one patient was experiencing 'anxiety' when seen pacing the corridors. When one pseudo-patient was observed writing, the staff recorded that the 'patient engages in writing behaviour'. The point here is that this subtly labels the 'writing behaviour' as odd and, therefore, confirms in some way a diagnosis of mental disorder.

Once admitted to hospital, the pseudopatients reported that they no longer heard any voices. After an average of nineteen days (with a range of 7–52 days), the staff appeared to be confident that the pseudopatients were well enough to be discharged. They had been prescribed a total of 2,100 pills. All of the patients were discharged with a diagnosis of schizophrenia in remission. As well as detailing the often inappropriate and inadequate treatment received by the pseudopatients, Rosenhan comments on the participants' impression that the only people who were apparently suspicious of the 'reality' of their mental illnesses were other patients, one of whom claimed that: 'You're not crazy, you're a journalist or a professor. You're checking up on the hospital.'

Rosenhan describes how he then revealed the findings of this initial phase of his study to some of his colleagues, and announced that more pseudopatients would try to gain admission to a particular teaching hospital during a particular three-month period. Each staff member was asked to make a judgement as to whether each new patient was an impostor or a 'real' patient. A total of 193 patients were admitted over the three-month period, of whom forty-one were confidently judged to be impostors by at least one member of staff. In fact, Rosenhan did not send any pseudopatients. All of those who presented themselves for admission were ordinary members of the public with 'genuine' reasons for distress.

Rosenhan's research has, I believe rightly, been widely reported. He observed and recorded the conditions and practices in psychiatric hospitals. It is relevant, for example, that staff members only spent 11 per cent of their time interacting with patients, and that comments like 'Come on, you motherf-----s, get out of bed' were reported as common. Despite the prescription of 2,100 pills, daily contact with psychiatrists, psychologists and nurses totalled only seven minutes.

However, the main claim from Rosenhan's study concerns the invalidity of diagnosis. In this case, despite some claims made concerning the study, the individuals did in fact provide the psychiatrists with what could be seen as reasonable grounds for acting as they did. According to DSM-IV, hearing auditory hallucinations is a symptom of schizophrenia. Psychiatrists believe that schizophrenia warrants hospital treatment and medication. Within the rubric of diagnosis and classification, such approaches are valid. However, they are not as valid within the psychological model I am attempting to outline here.

One could conclude that the psychiatrists and nurses followed the logic of their system, but that the system itself is invalid. Psychologists would advocate exploring the degree to which a person was distressed by hearing the word 'thud', what it meant to them and how the experience affected and was influenced by the rest of the person's life. On the basis of this, a decision could be made to suggest help, and that could even include hospitalisation and medication. In the case of Rosenhan's pseudopatients, many clinical psychologists now would probably offer reassurance and explanation.

I haven't conducted a partial replication of Rosenhan's experiment, but I was involved in a recent BBC *Horizon* programme – 'How mad are you?' [13] – that looked at the same issue. We took ten normal (but quite extrovert) individuals, five of whom were currently receiving help for mental health problems (and who had received diagnoses from very reputable psychiatrists), and five of whom had experienced no such problems. We put these ten rather brave individuals through a series of stressful experiences: clearing the slurry in a cow-byre, an orienteering challenge, performing stand-up comedy, a paint-balling challenge, and a series of psychological tests. The aim was to let a panel of experts – a psychiatrist (in fact, the psychiatrist who had developed the standard psychiatric diagnostic interview), a clinical psychologist and a nurse – look at the individuals' performance on these tasks (which were filmed by the BBC) and attempt to sort the ten into two groups: those with and those without mental health problems; and, if possible, to identify the diagnoses.

In strict scientific terms, the reliability of these decisions – the division into two groups and the individual diagnoses – would always be low. The panel of experts did not interview, or see interviews with, the participants, and the obvious questions (such as 'do you experience low mood most of the day, nearly every day?') were not asked. However, this wasn't a scientific experiment: the purpose was to explore the validity, the meaningfulness, of these diagnoses. The question was: do these diagnoses have any bearing on a person's experience in real life?

Our 'diagnostic' experiences were designed for TV. A paint-balling competition is not a standard means of obtaining a diagnosis, but it serves to illustrate a point – the expert panellists could not identify those individuals who had and those who didn't have a diagnosis of mental health problems and, consequently, who was in receipt of help. As someone who experiences considerable social anxiety, but who has never (unlike one of the participants) received a diagnosis of social anxiety 'disorder', I felt great admiration for one of my colleagues when faced with a stand-up comedy challenge. Of course, some performed better than others, but the presence of a diagnosis of a mental health 'disorder' seemed to make little difference. The expert judges were not able to tell which participants had received psychiatric diagnoses even when watching people attempting stand-up comedy. Most remarkably, they were unable to identify which of the participants had received a diagnosis of 'social anxiety disorder' when on stage, performing in public. What is the benefit of diagnosis, then?

THERAPEUTIC VALIDITY

Many of my psychiatric colleagues understand these arguments but argue that, despite their flaws, diagnoses are useful. They point out that diagnoses help us to communicate and guide treatment, and the usefulness of a diagnosis is in its ability to cast light on the causes of a person's symptoms. For example, a diagnosis of 'malaria' would suggest that the individual has suffered a particular infection, and even that the person has recently travelled to tropical countries. It also tells you which treatment is likely to help and what the prognosis is. Similar predictions have never been very successful in psychiatry, and particularly poor in the case of psychosis.

If a diagnosis is valid, it should indicate prognosis. However, the outcomes for people's diagnoses other than those for learning disability or neurological disease are extremely variable, and all the attempts at revision of the diagnostic criteria have been less than perfectly successful.

Diagnoses should also indicate what treatments will be effective. However, it appears that it is difficult to predict what treatment people will benefit from on the basis of the diagnosis they receive, and treatments often appear to be given for reasons other than those based on diagnosis.

More importantly, responses to medication for diagnostic categories such 'schizophrenia' and 'bipolar disorder' are also variable; for example, the drugs known as 'neuroleptics' or 'antipsychotics', commonly used as specific treatments for schizophrenia. However, not everyone with a diagnosis of schizophrenia seems to benefit significantly, while some people with other diagnoses (traditionally thought of as unrelated to 'schizophrenia') do benefit from these drugs. The effectiveness of lithium, a drug traditionally used with people diagnosed as suffering from bipolar disorder, is similarly variable and non-specific. In one study, the researchers examined people who had received either a neuroleptic, lithium, both or neither, and who had also received a diagnosis of either schizophrenia or bipolar disorder. It was found that drug response was related to specific problems but not diagnoses: delusions and hallucinations responded to the neuroleptic and mood swings responded to the lithium, irrespective of diagnosis. The traditional medical approach is to base treatment on diagnosis – and much of the argument in favour of the diagnostic approach stresses this. Since psychiatric diagnosis doesn't appear to be very helpful in guiding treatment, this seems a rather fatal problem.

Diagnosis also fails to help when it comes to predicting violence. Very few people with diagnoses of mental illnesses commit violent acts, including homicide (murder and manslaughter). However, only 5 per cent of homicides are committed by psychiatric patients and most psychiatric patients are not dangerous. Moreover, specific diagnoses such as 'schizophrenia' do not predict how dangerous someone is. Again, diagnostic categories are therefore of very limited use in predicting course or outcome; in fact, especially when it comes to violence, individual problems (such as a history of violent behaviour) are better at predicting future violence than are diagnoses.

STATISTICAL VALIDITY

Another way of examining the validity of diagnostic categories involves using statistical techniques to investigate whether people's psychotic experiences actually do cluster together in the way predicted by the diagnostic approach. The results of this research have not generally supported the validity of distinct diagnostic categories. Psychotic symptoms do not appear to correlate with each other in a manner that would reflect the diagnostic categories, for example. Similarly, cluster analysis – a statistical technique for assigning people to groups according to particular characteristics – has shown that the problems reported by psychiatric patients do not reflect commonly recognised diagnostic groups. Statistical techniques have also highlighted the considerable overlap between those diagnosed with schizophrenia and those diagnosed as having other 'disorders' – both in scientific analyses and in the diagnostic criteria themselves.

  In 2009, a doctoral student, Gemma Parker, Simon Duff and myself looked at the statistical validity of diagnoses using a statistical technique called smallest space analysis.[14] This is a highly technical method of looking at how each particular experience (in this case the presence or absence of a symptom of a psychiatric diagnosis) correlates with every other experience in a particular sample. Gemma interviewed forty-four people,